MULTIMODAL INTERACTIVE
HANDWRITTEN TEXT
TRANSCRIPTION

SERIES IN MACHINE PERCEPTION AND ARTIFICIAL INTELLIGENCE*

Editors: **H. Bunke** (Univ. Bern, Switzerland)
P. S. P. Wang (Northeastern Univ., USA)

*For the complete list of titles in this series, please write to the Publisher.

Series in Machine Perception and Artificial Intelligence – Vol. 80

MULTIMODAL INTERACTIVE HANDWRITTEN TEXT TRANSCRIPTION

Verónica Romero
Alejandro Héctor Toselli
Enrique Vidal

Universitat Politècnica de València, Spain

World Scientific

NEW JERSEY · LONDON · SINGAPORE · BEIJING · SHANGHAI · HONG KONG · TAIPEI · CHENNAI

Published by

World Scientific Publishing Co. Pte. Ltd.

5 Toh Tuck Link, Singapore 596224

USA office: 27 Warren Street, Suite 401-402, Hackensack, NJ 07601

UK office: 57 Shelton Street, Covent Garden, London WC2H 9HE

British Library Cataloguing-in-Publication Data
A catalogue record for this book is available from the British Library.

Series in Machine Perception and Artificial Intelligence — Vol. 80
MULTIMODAL INTERACTIVE HANDWRITTEN TEXT TRANSCRIPTION

Copyright © 2012 by World Scientific Publishing Co. Pte. Ltd.

ISBN-13 978-981-4390-33-0
ISBN-10 981-4390-33-X

Printed in Singapore by B & Jo Enterprise Pte Ltd

Preface

Handwritten Text Recognition (HTR) is not a new field of pattern recognition. In fact, HTR had its beginnings in the late 1960s with the recognition of zip codes on letter envelopes or account and amount information on checks. However, the available technologies or the computer capacity of those days were not enough for large scale HTR and, therefore, early research and development efforts focused on OCR (Optical Character Recognition). As its name implies, OCR deals with the recognition of individual, isolated characters, generally using simple, straightforward pattern recognition classification techniques. HTR should not be confused with OCR, because it is generally impossible to reliably isolate the characters or even the words that compose a cursive handwritten text, thereby rendering OCR classification technology completely useless. To some extent HTR is comparable with the task of recognizing continuous speech in a significantly degraded audio file. And, in fact, the nowadays prevalent technology for HTR borrows concepts and methods, such as Hidden Markov Models (HMMs) and N-grams, from the field of Automatic Speech Recognition (ASR).

For some time in the past decades, the interest in HTR was diminishing, under the assumption that modern computer technologies should soon make paper-based text documents useless. However, more recently, HTR has became an important research topic, specially because of the increasing number of on-line archives and digital libraries publishing large quantities of digitized legacy documents. The vast majority of these documents, thousands of terabytes worth of digital image data, remain waiting to be transcribed into a textual electronic format that would provide historians and other researchers new ways of indexing, consulting and querying these documents.

Given the difficult kind of handwritten text images involved in old documents, the results provided by the currently available automatic text recognition technologies are far from offering perfect solutions to this transcription problem. Typically, modern, HTR technologies produce word error rates as high as 20-60% with unrestricted text images. Clearly, to obtain perfect transcriptions, the only possibility to use these systems is by acknowledging the need of a human-expert intervention to revise or *"post-edit"* the system results. This post-editing solution is quite inefficient and uncomfortable to the users and it is not generally accepted by expert transcribers, who often prefer to type by themselves all the transcription rather than check and correct the text produced by HTR system; clearly, by post-editing the output of the HTR system, paleography experts feel they are not in command of the transcription process.

An interactive scenario, where the automatic HTR system and the human transcriber cooperate to generate the final transcription of the text images, offers promise for significant improvements in practical performance and user acceptance. The rationale behind this approach is to combine the accuracy provided by the transcriber with the efficiency of the HTR system. This fits within a framework of developing machines to assist human beings in their works, instead of fully automatic devices. This framework has been previously applied in fields such as machine translation and speech transcription, where experiments and real field tests have shown that, by capitalizing on the human feedback, interactive systems can save significant amounts of overall human effort. On the one hand, the feedback can lead to great human/machine performance improvements, provided it is adequately taken into account in the mathematical formulation under which systems are developed. On the other hand, interactive processing allows the human user to feel in command of the system, rather than the other way around.

This book is the result of work carried out in the development of an interactive multimodal approach for accurate and efficient transcription of handwritten text images. Most of this work was carried out as part of the doctoral thesis [Romero (2010)]. More precisely, this book covers three groups of topics as follows:

(1) **Computer assisted operation.** An interactive predictive scenario, previously studied in machine translation and speech transcription, is applied to the handwritten text recognition problem.
(2) **Response time.** The system must be able to interact with the human expert in a time efficient way, otherwise the user will prefer to transcribe

the document without any help. Therefore, good responsiveness is critical. We study different implementations to obtain a good response time without a significant loss in accuracy.

(3) **Ergonomics and multimodal interaction.** Several ideas are explored aiming to make the interaction process friendly and ergonomic to the user. We develop and assess a multimodal computer assisted transcription system which takes advantage of feedback data naturally provided by conventional keyboard and mouse interfaces. Moreover, feedback derived from electronic pen (e-pen) multimodal communication is estudied and evaluated.

The above topics are studied in 7 chapters. Chap. 1 provides an introduction to the transcription problem and an overview of the state-of-the-art in OCR and HTR. Later, background, formulation and algorithms related with HMMs, n-gram language models, multimodal interactive pattern recognition and word-graphs are presented.

In Chap. 2 the data sets used in the experiments are introduced. We use three off-line handwritten data sets and one on-line handwritten corpus.

A detailed description of the baseline HTR systems is given in Chap. 3. These systems follow a classical Pattern Recognition architecture composed of three modules: preprocessing, feature extraction and recognition. All these modules are studied and assessed with the corpora described on Chap. 2.

In Chap. 4, computer assisted HTR is introduced and assessed on the three off-line handwritten corpora presented in Chap. 2. In order to improve the quality and ergonomy of the interactive process, different ways to interact with the system using the keyboard and the mouse are presented, including mouse-click and character level interaction. To improve the response time, two different approaches to implement the decoding process are also derived and assessed on the same off-line handwritten tasks.

A multimodal version of the interactive system studied in Chap. 4 is presented and evaluated in Chap. 5. E-pen communication is the modality adopted to obtain an easier and more comfortable human-machine interaction. Decoding the e-pen feedback signals amounts to on-line HTR. The on-line feedback decoding subsystem uses the same baseline technology used in the case of the baseline off-line HTR. This technology is based on HMMs and n-gram language models, as outlined in Chap. 3. Different ways to fuse the off-line and the on-line modalities are studied and assessed, using the datasets presented in Chap. 2.

Chap. 6 addresses the implementation of the approaches studied in previous sections. In particular, a web-based demonstrator for interactive transcription of handwritten text images is described and assessed with real users.

In Chap. 7, a summary of the work and contributions presented in this book are discussed, followed by an outlook of possible research directions.

Finally, a list of mathematical symbols and acronyms used throughout this book is presented in Appendix A.

Verónica Romero, Alejandro H. Toselli and Enrique Vidal

Contents

Chapter 1

Preliminaries

1.1 Introduction

In recent years, the Pattern Recognition (PR) paradigm has been shifting from the concept of full-automaton, i.e. systems where no human intervention is assumed, to systems where the decision process is affected by human feedback. One remarkable PR example where this feedback can be advantageously used is handwritten document transcription. The increasing number of on-line digital libraries publishing large quantities of digitized legacy documents has turned this task into an important research topic. The vast majority of these documents, thousands of terabytes worth of digital image data, remain waiting to be transcribed into a textual electronic format that would provide historians and other researchers new ways of indexing, consulting and querying.

The transcription of these documents is usually carried out by experts in paleography, who are specialized in reading ancient scripts, characterized, among other things, by different calligraphy/print styles from diverse places and time periods. How long experts take to carry out a transcription of one of these documents depends on their skills and experience, as well as on the type of text and the quality of the documents to be transcribed. For example, to transcribe many of the pages of the documents used in the experiments presented in this book, they would typically spend more than half an hour per page.

State-of-the-art cursive handwritten text recognition (HTR) systems can by no means substitute the experts in this task. HTR systems have indeed proven useful for restricted applications involving form-constrained handwriting and/or fairly limited vocabulary (such as postal addresses or bank check legal amounts), achieving in this kind of tasks relatively high recognition accuracy [Srihari and Keubert (1997); Dimauro *et al.* (2002)]. However, in the case of unconstrained handwritten documents (such as old manuscripts and/or unconstrained, spontaneous text), current HTR technology typically only achieves results which are far from being directly acceptable in practice.

Therefore, once the full recognition process of one of these documents has finished, heavy human expert revision is required to really produce a transcription of standard quality. The human transcriber is, therefore, responsible for verifying and correcting the mistakes made by the system. In this context, the transcription process is performed "in-batch". First, the HTR system returns a full transcription of all the text lines in the whole document. Next, the human transcriber reads this sequentially (while looking at their correspondences in the original page images) and corrects the mistakes made by the system. Given the high error rates involved, such a *post-editing* solution is quite inefficient and uncomfortable for the human corrector, who often prefers to carry out the transcription without using any kind of HTR system.

An *interactive* scenario allows for a more effective approach. This book studies innovative technologies to implement *computer assisted* solutions. These technologies are based on a recently introduced framework called "interactive predictive processing" [Vidal *et al.* (2007b); Toselli *et al.* (2011)]. In this framework the automatic HTR system and the human transcriber cooperate to generate the final transcription of the text images. The rationale behind this approximation is to combine the accuracy provided by the transcription expert with the efficiency of the HTR system. We call this approach "Computer Assisted Transcription of Text Images" (CATTI). It follows similar ideas as those previously applied to computer assisted translation [Civera *et al.* (2004a); Barrachina *et al.* (2009)] and speech transcription [Rodríguez *et al.* (2007); Vidal *et al.* (2007b)], where experiments and real field tests have shown that, by capitalizing on the human feedback, this kind of systems can save significant amounts of overall human effort. In this approach, at each interaction step, the system proposes its best output for the given input data (e.g., its best transcription for the given text line image). If the user finds it correct, then it is accepted and the process goes on with successive input data. Otherwise, the user introduces some information that the system takes into account in order to improve the proposed transcription.

This scenario is fundamentally different from the (generally unsatisfactory) non-interactive post-editing solution in at least two relevant aspects.

First, the fact that the user is involved in the system transcription process provides a much more friendly environment, letting the user be in command of the system, rather than the other way around. And second, the effort needed by the user to obtain a perfect transcription of the input handwritten text image can be significantly smaller. This is thanks to the direct pay-off obtained by taking advantage of the user feedback information to immediately improve system results. That is, when the user amends some erroneous element found in the system output, the system reacts with a revised output where not only this error is fixed, but other subsequent, related errors can be corrected.

Another important aspect of this work is *multimodal processing*. As will be discussed later, human feedback signals in interactive systems rarely belong to the same domain as the one the main data stream comes from, thereby entailing some sort of *multimodality*. Of course, this is the case in CATTI, where the main data are text images and feedback would consists of keystrokes and/or pointer positioning actions. Nevertheless, at the expense of loosing the deterministic accuracy of the traditional keyboard and mouse, more ergonomic multimodal interfaces are possible. It is worth noting, however, that the potential increase in user-friendliness comes at the cost of acknowledging new possible errors coming from the decoding of the feedback signals. Therefore, solving the *multimodal interaction problem* amounts to achieving a *modality synergy* where both main and feedback data streams help each-other to optimize overall accuracy. These ideas have recently been explored in the context of computer assisted translation, using speech signals for feedback [Vidal *et al.* (2007a,b)].

Among many possible feedback modalities for CATTI, we focus here on touch-screen operation, which is perhaps the most natural modality to provide the required feedback in CATTI systems. Figure 1.1 (top) shows a user interacting with a CATTI system by means of a touch-screen. Both the original text image and the successive *off-line* HTR system's transcription hypotheses can be easily aligned and jointly displayed on the touchscreen, as shown in Fig. 1.1 (bottom). This way, the user corrective feedback can be quite naturally provided by means of pen strokes, exactly registered over the text produced by the system, which are fed to an *on-line* HTR subsystem. We will use the shorthand "MM-CATTI" for this kind of *multimodal* CATTI processing. Touchscreen devices are very popular human-computer interfaces for editing tasks. For instance, in [Suhm *et al.* (2001)] and [Liu and Soong (2006)], they are considered for (non-interactive) post-editing and for interactively correcting the output of a speech recognizer.

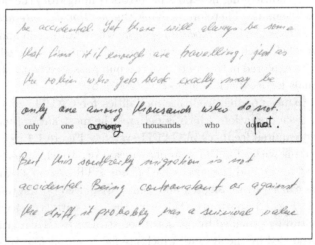

Fig. 1.1 Top: illustration of CATTI multimodal user-interaction using a touch-screen. Bottom: page fragment showing a line image being processed, with the corrections made by the user through pen strokes and handwriting input marked in black.

Interestingly, a uniform technology, based on Hidden Markov Models (HMMs) can be used both for the main *off-line* HTR system and for the *on-line* feedback HTR subsystem. HMMs are used in the same way as they are used in current automatic speech recognition (ASR) systems [Jelinek (1998)]. The most important differences lay in the type of input feature vectors sequences; while they represent acoustic data in the case of ASR, line-image features and point coordinates of handwritten pen strokes constitute the input sequences for off- and on-line HTR, respectively.

In this book we study the CATTI framework and its multimodal version, MM-CATTI. We also present comprehensive experiments carried out to assess the capabilities of CATTI and MM-CATTI.

In this chapter, first we overview the state-of-the-art of OCR and HTR systems in Sec. 1.2. Next, the bases, formulations and algorithms related with HMM, n-grams, Interactive Pattern Recognition and word-graphs are enunciated in Sec. 1.3. Finally, the assessment criteria followed in this book is presented in Sec. 1.4

1.2 State of the Art

Many documents used every day are handwritten documents, as for example, postal addresses, bank checks, medical prescriptions, a huge quantity of historical documents, an important part of the information gathered in forms, etc. In many cases it would be interesting to have these documents in digital-text form rather than as raw images, in order to allow for indexing, consulting and working with them.

Handwriting text recognition (HTR) can be defined as the ability of a computer to transform handwritten input represented in its spatial form of graphical marks into an equivalent symbolic representation as ASCII text. Usually, this handwritten input comes from sources such as paper documents, photographs or electronic pens and touch-screens.

HTR is a relatively new field of computer vision. Optical character recognition (OCR) had its beginnings in the year 1951 with the optical reader invented by David H. Shepard. This reader, known as GISMO, was able to read typewritten text, morse and musical notes [Shepard (1953)]. HTR first appeared in the late 1960s with restricted applications involving very limited vocabulary, such as the recognition of postal addresses or bank checks. The computer capacity and the available technology of those days was not enough for unconstrained handwritten documents (such as old manuscripts and/or unconstrained, spontaneous text). Even the recognition of printed text was only adequate on simplified fonts, for example the font used on credit cards ever since. However, the increase in computers capacity nowadays, the development of adequate technologies and the necessity of processing automatically big quantities of handwritten documents, have brought handwritten text recognition to an important focus of attention both to industry as well as to the research community, leading recently to significant accuracy improvements.

According to [Bunke *et al.* (1995); Bertolami and Bunke (2008)], current OCR systems can recognize typed text in several fonts with good accuracy. However, to achieve high recognition accuracy for continuous, cursive handwritten text is still a challenging problem. It is mainly due to the high variability in handwriting styles and in the difficulty of word and character segmentation.

Both OCR and HTR systems involve two different phases: training and recognition. Usually, training is carried out in the laboratory, where the different preprocessing operations, the different features and the classification methods are studied in order to choose those that obtain better results. If the labels of the samples used for training are known we speak of *supervised learning*. However, if only unlabelled examples are given the training is called *unsupervised learning*. Unlike training, recognition is the operative phase of the system, where unknown samples that arrive to the system are recognized.

1.2.1   *Optical Character Recognition*

Optical character recognition, usually abbreviated as OCR, is the mechanical translation of images of handwritten, typewritten or printed discrete text elements (letters, numbers or symbols) into machine-editable symbols. Historic reviews of OCR can be found in [Mori *et al.* (1992); Impedovo *et al.* (1991)]. Big improvements in the recognition of printed text have been achieved until now, based on the easy to segment the text into characters. This improvement has made it possible the development of OCR systems with a very good accuracy, close to 99% at the character level.

In the OCR field, recognition is performed using one or several classifiers. A naive but quite effective approach to the recognition of an image containing a single symbol is the nearest neighbour (NN) or k-NN classifier. More sophisticated algorithms which may achieve better results are artificial neural networks (ANNs) and support vector machines (SVMs) [Lee (1996);

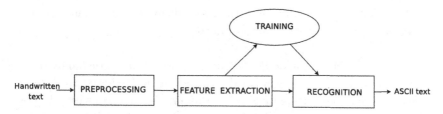

Fig. 1.2   Diagram representing the different modules of an handwritten text recognition system.

Srihari (1993)]. Moreover, some work has been carried out using tangent vectors and local representations [Keysers *et al.* (2002)] or Bernoulli mixture models [Juan and Vidal (2001); Romero *et al.* (2007b); Giménez *et al.* (2010)] with good results. Lately, some works that post-process the results of an OCR system taking into account lexical and syntactical information have been presented with good results [Pérez-Cortes *et al.* (2000); Llobet *et al.* (2010)].

However, given the kind of text image documents we are interested in this book, OCR products, or even the most advanced OCR research prototypes [Ratzlaff (2003)], are very far from offering useful solutions to the handwritten transcription problem. They are simply not usable since, in the vast majority of the handwritten text images of interest, characters can by no means be pre-isolated automatically.

1.2.2   *Handwritten Text Recognition*

HTR can be considered a relatively new field on PR. An overview of the state-of-the-art can be found on [Kim *et al.* (1999); Plamondon and Srihari (2000); Vinciarelli (2002); Plötz and Fink (2009)]. In [Bunke (2003)] a detailed description of what has been made so far and the possible progress in a near future is given.

Essentially, modern HTR systems follow a classical pattern recognition (PR) architecture composed of three modules (see Fig. 1.2):

- **Acquisition and preprocessing module:** in charge of acquiring and preprocessing the data. Here noise is filtered out, the handwritten strokes from degraded images are recovered and the variability of the text styles is reduced.
- **Feature extraction module:** a feature vector sequence is obtained as the representation of the handwritten text.

- **Recognition module:** here the most likely word sequence for the sequence of feature vectors is obtained.

According to the mode of data acquisition used, automatic handwriting recognition systems can be classified into *on-line* and *off-line*. In *Off-line* systems the handwriting data are given as images of text, without time sequence information. In *On-line* systems the handwriting data consists of temporal sequences of coordinates that represent pen tip trajectories. In this book the main system considered (for CATTI, see Chap. 4) is an *off-line* system. However, the feedback provided by the user (in the MM-CATTI, see Chap. 5) comes in the form of *on-line* data.

Many past efforts in the development of off-line handwriting transcription systems relied on technology for isolated character recognition (OCR) developed in previous decades. First, the input image is segmented into characters or pieces of a character. Thereafter, isolated character recognition is performed on these segments. In [Bozinovic and Srihari (1989); Kavallieratou *et al.* (2002); Senior and Robinson (1998)] this approximation is followed, using segmentation techniques based on dynamic programming. As it was previously explained, the difficulty of this approach is the segmentation step. In fact, the difficulty of character segmentation for most handwritten documents, usually renders this approach infeasible.

The required technology should be able to recognize all text elements (sentences, words and characters) as a whole, without any prior segmentation of the image into these elements. This technology is generally referred to as "holistic" or "segmentation-free" off-line Handwritten Text Recognition. Nowadays, HMM technology is widely used in segmentation-free recognizers such as [Bazzi *et al.* (1999); Plamondon and Srihari (2000); Marti and Bunke (2001); Koerich *et al.* (2003); Toselli *et al.* (2004b); Romero *et al.* (2007a); Plötz and Fink (2009)]. Recently, HTR systems based on hybrid HMM [España Boquera *et al.* (2011)] and Artificial Neural Networks [Graves *et al.* (2009)] have been proposed with good results.

However, the results obtained with these systems are still very far from offering usable accuracy. For (high quality, modern) unrestricted text images, current HTR state-of-the-art (research) prototypes provide accuracy levels that range from 40 to 80% at the word level. This fact has lead us to propose the development of the computer-assisted solutions based on novel interactive-predictive approaches presented through this book.

Before closing this subsection, we should mention that current on-line handwriting transcription systems are more accurate than off-line systems.

The timing information included in the coordinate sequences allows for significantly higher recognition accuracy. In fact, current on-line HTR results are considered sufficiently accurate for many on-line text-input applications [Manke *et al.*; Parizeau *et al.* (2001); Jaeger *et al.* (2001)], reaching 90% word-level accuracy in favourable cases.

1.3 Formal Background

This section gives an overview of the theoretical foundation of the recognition process. Here the theoretical bases, formulations and main algorithms related with HMMs and *n*-grams are revised. These statistical models are the basis of the systems developed on this work. Then, we focus on interactive pattern recognition. Finally, the word-graphs technology, used in the CATTI and MM-CATTI systems, is introduced.

1.3.1 *Hidden Markov Models*

A Hidden Markov Model (HMM) is a finite set of states, each of which is associated with a (generally continuous, multidimensional) probability distribution of "observations". Transitions among the states are governed by a set of probabilities called transition probabilities. In a particular state an outcome or observation can be generated, according to the associated probability distribution. Only the outcomes, not the states are visible to an external observer and therefore states are "hidden" to the outside; hence the name Hidden Markov Model.

During the past decades it has become the most successful model used in Automatic Speech Recognition (ASR). The main reason for this success is its wonderful ability to characterize the speech signal in a mathematically tractable way. In ASR, HMM observations are discrete time sequences of acoustic parameter vectors. Given the similarity between ASR and HTR, the HMMs have seen increased their popularity in the HTR community. In HTR, the HMM observations are also discrete time sequences. However, in this case, the observations represent line-image features or point coordinates of handwritten pen strokes.

HMMs can be classified according to the nature of the observations. When the observations are symbols in a finite alphabet we are speaking of discrete HMMs. Another possibility is to work with continuous observations; the HMMs used in this case are called continuous HMMs. Finally, the third class is called semi-continuous HMMs. These models use discrete observations, but they are modelled using continuous probability density functions [Jelinek (1998); Lee (1989)] .

Since in this book we work with continuous HMMs, the formal definition and the formulation related with this kind of HMMs is summarized in the next subsections.

Continuous HMM

Here, a formal definition of a continuous HMM is given, using similar notation presented in [Toselli (2004)]. We assume that the observations can be only generated at states and not in the transitions. Moreover, one additional initial state, which does not emit any observation, has been defined, in a similar way as in the case of the end state.

Both in ASR and HTR, HMMs are used to compute the probability of the input signal represented as a sequence of feature vectors. Let be $\mathbf{x} = \vec{x}_1\vec{x}_2...\vec{x}_T$, a sequence of real vectors, a HMM M approximates the probability of this sequence; that is[1]:

$$\Pr(\mathbf{x}) \approx P_M(\mathbf{x}) \tag{1.1}$$

Formally, a continuous HMM is a finite state machine defined by the sextuple (Q, I, F, X, a, b) where:

- Q is a finite set of states. In order to avoid confusions with the indexation of the different states, we denote the states of the model as $q_0, ..., q_{|Q|-1}$, whereas a sequence of states that generates the vector sequence $\mathbf{x} = \vec{x}_1\vec{x}_2...\vec{x}_T$ will be denoted as $z_1z_2...z_T$.
- I is the initial state, an element of Q: $I \in Q$. $I = q_0$
- F is the final state, an element of Q: $F \in Q$. $F = q_{|Q|-1}$
- X is a real d-dimensional space of observations: $X \subseteq \Re^d$.
- a is the state-transition probability function:

$$a(q_i, q_j) = P(z_{t+1} = q_j | z_t = q_i) \quad q_i \in (Q - \{F\}), \quad q_j \in (Q - \{I\})$$

where $z_t = q_i$ means that the HMM is in the state q_i at time t. Transition probabilities should satisfy $a(q_i, q_j) \geq 0$ and

$$\sum_{q_j \in (Q-\{I\})} a(q_i, q_j) = 1 \quad \forall q_i \in (Q - \{F\})$$

---

[1] "True" probabilities are written as $\Pr(...)$, in contrast with model approximations such as $P_M(z \mid ...)$ which, to simplify notation, will be denoted as $P(z \mid ...)$ whenever M can be understood

- b is a probability distribution function[2]:

$$b(q_i, \vec{x}) = P(\vec{x}_t = \vec{x} | z_t = q_i) \quad q_i \in (Q - \{I, F\}), \quad \vec{x} \in X$$

The following stochastic constraints must be satisfied: $b(q_i, \vec{x}) \geq 0$ and

$$\int_{\vec{x} \in X} b(q_i, \vec{x}) d\vec{x} = 1 \quad \forall q_i \in (Q - \{I, F\})$$

As the observations are continuous then we use a continuous probability density function. In this case it is defined as a weighted sum of G Gaussian distributions:

$$b(q_j, \vec{x}) = \sum_{g=1}^{G} c_{jg} b_g(q_j, \vec{x})$$

where,

$$b_g(q_j, \vec{x}) = \frac{1}{\sqrt{(2\pi)^d |\Sigma_{jg}|}} e^{(-\frac{1}{2}(\vec{x} - \mu'_{jg}) \Sigma_{jg}^{-1} (\vec{x} - \mu_{jg}))}$$

- μ_{jg} is the mean vector for the component g of the state q_j
- Σ_{jg} is the covariance matrix for the component g of the state q_j
- c_{jg} is the weighting coefficient for the component g of the state q_j, and should satisfy the stochastic constrain $c_{jg} \geq 0$ and

$$\sum_{g=1}^{G} c_{jg} = 1$$

For the sake of mathematical and computational tractability, the following assumptions are made in the theory of HMMs:

(1) **The Markov assumption.** As given in the definition of HMMs, transition probabilities are defined as: $a(q_i, q_j) = P(z_{t+1} = q_j | z_t = q_i)$. In other words it is assumed that the next state is dependent only upon the current state; that is,

$$\Pr(z_{t+1} | z_1 ... z_t) \approx P(z_{t+1} | z_t)$$

It is called the Markov assumption and the resulting model becomes actually a first order HMM.

(2) **The stationary assumption.** Here it is assumed that state transition probabilities are independent of the actual time at which the transitions takes place. Mathematically,

$$P(z_{t_1+1} = q_j | z_{t_1} = q_i) = P(z_{t_2+1} = q_j | z_{t_2} = q_i)$$

for any t_1 and t_2

---

[2]$\vec{x}_t = \vec{x}$ means that the HMM in the state z_t generates $\vec{x}$ at time t

(3) **The output independence assumption.** The probability distribution function is defined as: $b(q_i, \vec{x}) = p(\vec{x}_t = \vec{x} | z_t = q_i)$. This means that the current output (observation) is statistically independent of the previous outputs (observations) and it only depends of the current state; that is,

$$\Pr(\vec{x}_t | \vec{x}_1 ... \vec{x}_{t-1}, z_1 ... z_t) \approx P(\vec{x}_t | z_t)$$

Basic algorithms for HMMs

Once we have a HMM, there are three problems of interest. The evaluation problem, the decoding problem and the learning problem.

- The Evaluation Problem. This problem consist in computing the probability $P(\mathbf{x})$; that is, the probability that the observations are generated by the model.
- The Decoding Problem. Given a HMM and a sequence of observations $\mathbf{x}$, the problem is to find the most likely state sequence in the model which produced the observations. In other words, the problem consists on find the hidden part of the HMM.
- The Learning Problem. Given a HMM and a sequence of observations $\mathbf{x}$, how should we adjust the model parameters in order to maximize the probability $P(\mathbf{x})$.

To simplify the notation, in the next sections, $a(q_i, q_j)$ will be written as a_{ij} and $b(q_i, x)$ as $b_i(x)$[3].

The Evaluation Problem and the Forward and Backward Algorithms

Let $\mathbf{x}$ be a sequence of real vectors and $Z = \{\mathbf{z} = z_1 z_2 ... z_T : z_k = q_i \in (Q - \{I, F\}), 1 \leq i \leq |Q| - 2\}$ a set of state sequences associated with the vector sequence $\mathbf{x}$. Then, the probability that $\mathbf{x}$ be generated by the HMM is:

$$P(\mathbf{x}) = \sum_{\mathbf{z} \in Z} \left(\prod_{i=1}^{T} a_{z_{i-1} z_i} b_{z_i}(\vec{x}_i) \right) a_{z_T F}$$

where z_0 is the initial state I: $z_0 = q_0 = I$.

---

[3]From now on, any kind of subsequence will be represented as $l_i ... l_j$ or as l_i^j, whenever it is convenient.

This calculation involves number of operations in the order of N^T, where N is the number of states of the model excluding the initial state, $N = |Q| - 1$ ($Q = \{q_0 = I, q_1, ..., q_{N-1}, q_N = F\}$), and T is the number of vectors of the sequence. This is very large even if the length of the sequence, T is moderate. Therefore we have to look for another method for this calculation.

The **Forward** algorithm is an efficient algorithm to compute $P(\mathbf{x})$. The time complexity order of this algorithm is: $O(|Q|^2 \cdot T)$; however, using a left-to-right HMM the complexity falls to $O(|Q| \cdot T)$. In this topology a transition between two states $q_i, q_j \in Q$ from the HMM, it is only possible if $j \geq i$.

The forward function $\alpha_j(t)$ for $0 < j < N$, is defined as the probability of the partial observation sequence $x_1 x_2 ... x_t$, when it terminates at the state j. Mathematically, $\alpha_j(t) = P(\mathbf{x}_1^t, q_j)$ and it can be expressed in a recursive way:

$$\alpha_j(t) = \begin{cases} a_{0j} b_j(x_1) & t = 1 \\ \left(\sum_{i=1}^{N-1} \alpha_i(t-1) a_{ij} \right) b_j(\vec{x}_t) & 1 < t \leq T \end{cases}$$

with the initial condition that $\alpha_0(1) = 1$. Using this recursion we can calculate the probability that the sequence $\mathbf{x}$ be emitted by the model M as:

$$P(\mathbf{x}) = P(\mathbf{x}_1^T) = \alpha_N(T) = \sum_{i=1}^{N-1} \alpha_i(T) a_{iN}$$

In a similar way we can define the **Backward** function $\beta_i(t)$ for $0 < i < N$, as the probability of the partial observation sequence $x_{t+1} x_{t+2} ... x_T$, given that the current state is i. Mathematically, $\beta_i(t) = P(\mathbf{x}_{t+1}^T | q_i)$ and it can be expressed on a recursive way:

$$\beta_i(t) = \begin{cases} a_{iN} & t = T \\ \sum_{j=1}^{N-1} a_{ij} b_j(\vec{x}_{t+1}) \beta_j(t+1) & 1 \leq t < T \end{cases}$$

with the initial condition that $\beta_N(T) = 1$. Using this recursion the probability that the sequence $\mathbf{x}$ be emitted by the model M can be calculated as:

$$P(\mathbf{x}) = P(\mathbf{x}_1^T) = \beta_0(1) = \sum_{j=1}^{N-1} a_{0j} b_j(x_1) \beta_j(1)$$

As in the backward algorithm the time complexity is: $O(|Q|^2 \cdot T)$, and using a left-to-right HMM the complexity falls to $O(|Q| \cdot T)$.

The Decoding Problem and the Viterbi Algorithm

In this case we want to find the most likely state sequence, $\mathbf{z} = z_1 z_2 ... z_T$, for a given sequence of observations, $\mathbf{x}$. The algorithm used here is commonly known as the Viterbi algorithm, which maximizes the joint probability of the observations and all possible sequence of states; that is $\max_{\mathbf{z}} P(\mathbf{x}, \mathbf{z})$. This algorithm is similar to the forward algorithm, but replacing the sum by the dominating term.

$$
v_j(t) = \begin{cases} a_{0j} b_j(x_1) & t = 1 \\ \left(\max_{i \in [1, N-1]} v_i(t-1) a_{ij} \right) b_j(\vec{x}_t) & 1 < t \leq T \end{cases}
$$

with the condition that $v_0(1) = 1$. $v_N(T)$ is the probability $\max_{\mathbf{z}} P(\mathbf{x}, \mathbf{z})$ and using this recursion it can be calculated as:

$$
v_N(T) = \max_{i \in [1, N-1]} v_i(T) a_{iN} \leq \sum_{i=1}^{N-1} \alpha_i(T) a_{iN} = \alpha_N(T)
$$

The time complexity of the Viterbi algorithm is: $O(|Q|^2 \cdot T)$, and using a left-to-right HMM the complexity falls to $O(|Q| \cdot T)$.

The Learning Problem and the Baum-Welch Algorithm

The learning problem is how to adjust the HMM parameters $(a_{ij}, b_i(x), c_{jg}, \mu_{jg}$ and $\Sigma_{jg})$, so that a given set of observations (called training set) is generated by the model with maximum likelihood. The Baum-Welch algorithm [Rabiner and Juang (1993)] (also known as Forward-Backward algorithm), is used to find these unknown parameters. It is an expectation-maximization (EM) algorithm.

Let $E = \{ \mathbf{x}_r = \vec{x}_{r1} \vec{x}_{r2} ... \vec{x}_{rT_r} : \vec{x}_{rk} \in X, 1 \leq k \leq T_r \wedge 1 \leq r \leq R \}$ a set of R vector sequences, used to adjust the HMM parameters. The basic formula to estimate the state-transition probability a_{ij} is:

$$
\hat{a}_{ij} = \frac{\sum_{r=1}^{R} \frac{1}{P_r} \sum_{t=1}^{T_r - 1} \alpha_i^r(t) a_{ij} b_j(\vec{x}_{rt+1}) \beta_j^r(t+1)}{\sum_{r=1}^{R} \frac{1}{P_r} \sum_{t=1}^{T_r} \alpha_i^r(t) \beta_i^r(t)}
$$

where $0 < i < N$, $0 < j < N$ and $P_r = P(\mathbf{x}_r)$ is the total probability of the sample r from the set E.

If the probability density function of each state on the HMM is approximated by a weighted sum of G Gaussian distributions we must find the unknown parameters c_{jg}, μ_{jg} and Σ_{jg}. With this purpose we define $L_{jg}^r(t)$

as the probability that the vector $\vec{x}_{rt} \in \Re^d$ be generated by the Gaussian component g in the q_j state:

$$L_{jg}^r(t) = \frac{1}{P_r} U_j^r(t) c_{jg} b_{jg}(\vec{x}_{rt}) \beta_j^r(t)$$

where

$$U_j^r(t) = \begin{cases} a_{0j} & if \quad t = 1 \\ \sum_{i=1}^{N-1} \alpha_i^r(t-1) a_{ij} & otherwise \end{cases}$$

Taking into account the previous definitions, the parameters c_{jg}, μ_{jg} and Σ_{jg} can be estimated as:

$$\hat{\mu}_{jg} = \frac{\sum_{r=1}^R \sum_{t=1}^{T_r} L_{jg}^r(t) \vec{x}_{rt}}{\sum_{r=1}^R \sum_{t=1}^{T_r} L_{jg}^r(t)}$$

$$\hat{\Sigma}_{jg} = \frac{\sum_{r=1}^R \sum_{t=1}^{T_r} L_{jg}^r(t)(\vec{x}_{rt} - \hat{\mu}_{jg})(\vec{x}_{rt} - \hat{\mu}_{jg})'}{\sum_{r=1}^R \sum_{t=1}^{T_r} L_{jg}^r(t)}$$

$$c_{jg} = \frac{\sum_{r=1}^R \sum_{t=1}^{T_r} L_{jg}^r(t)}{\sum_{r=1}^R \sum_{t=1}^{T_r} L_j^r(t)}$$

The time complexity of one iteration of the Baum-Welch algorithm is: $O(R \cdot |Q|^2 \cdot T)$; however, using a left-to-right HMM the complexity falls to $O(R \cdot |Q| \cdot T)$. This algorithm is iterated until some convergence criterion is reached.

Sometimes, it is necessary to have a composition of C HMM joined sequentially, for example in the case of the different letters that conform a sentence. In this case, the "embedded training Baum-Welch" algorithm, which re-estimates the parameters of the composition of C sequentially concatenated HMMs, can be used. This algorithm enables to train the HMM without any prior segmentation of the training images into word or characters. In [Toselli (2004)] we can find all the formula to compute the unknown parameters in this case.

1.3.2 *Language models: N-grams*

Language models (LMs) are used to model text properties, like syntax and semantic, independently from the character morphology modelled by HMMs. They are used in many natural language processing applications such as speech recognition, machine translation or handwritten recognition. These models can be used to predict the next word in a word sequence. Language models assign a probability to a sequence of words $\mathbf{w} = w_1, w_2, ..., w_l$, which can be expressed as:

$$\Pr(\mathbf{w}) = \Pr(w_1) \cdot \prod_{i=2}^{l} \Pr(w_i | \mathbf{w}_1^{i-1})$$

where $\Pr(w_i | \mathbf{w}_1^{i-1})$ is the probability of the word w_i when we have already seen the sequence of words $w_1 ... w_{i-1}$. The sequence of words prior to w_i is called history.

In practice, estimating the probability of sequences can become difficult since sentences can be arbitrarily long and hence many sequences are not observed during LM training. It is necessary to note that for a vocabulary with $|V|$ different words, the number of different histories is $|V|^{i-1}$. So, the estimation of $\Pr(\mathbf{w})$ can be unworkable. For that reason these models are often approximated using smoothed n-gram models, which obtain surprisingly good performance although they only capture short term dependencies.

An n-gram defines a function: $\Phi_n : V^* \to V^{n-1}$ in which, all sequences finishing with the same $n-1$ words belong to the same equivalence class. Now, $\Pr(\mathbf{w})$ can be approximated as:

$$\Pr(\mathbf{w}) \approx \prod_{i=1}^{l} P(w_i | \Phi_n(\mathbf{w}_1^{i-1})) = \prod_{i=1}^{l} P(w_i | \mathbf{w}_{i-n+1}^{i-1}) \tag{1.2}$$

Owing to the fact that $i - n \leq 0$ for the first $n-1$ words in $\mathbf{w}$, Eq. (1.2) must be written as:

$$\Pr(\mathbf{w}) \approx P(w_1) \cdot \prod_{i=2}^{n-1} P(w_i | \mathbf{w}_1^{i-1}) \cdot \prod_{i=n}^{l} P(w_i | \mathbf{w}_{i-n+1}^{i-1})) \tag{1.3}$$

Given a vocabulary V and a transcribed training data or text corpora represented by $\mathbf{w} = w_1 w_2 ... w_l$, the estimated probability of the word $v \in V$, having seen a sequence of $n-1$ words $\mathbf{v} \in V^{n-1}$, is computed as:

$$P(v|\mathbf{v}) = \frac{C(\mathbf{v}v)}{C(\mathbf{v})}$$

where $C(\mathbf{v})$ is the number of times that the sequence $\mathbf{v}$ has appeared in the training sequence $\mathbf{w}$. This is a maximum likelihood (ML) estimate.

Since not all possible n-grams have typically been seen in training, some smoothing method must be used to allow for unseen n-grams in the recognition phase. Two main smoothing techniques are: interpolation [Jelinek

(1998)] and "Back-off" [Katz (1987)]. In this book we are going to pay attention to the "Back-off" method.

The method presented by Katz consists in discounting a small mass of probability from the seen events, and to distribute it among the unseen events, or those that have been seen very few times, using a $(n-1)$-gram model also smoothed by "back-off". This is a recursive function that can be expressed as:

$$\hat{P}_{bo}(v_i \mid \mathbf{v}_{i-n+1}^{i-1}) = \begin{cases} f(v_i \mid \mathbf{v}_{i-n+1}^{i-1}) & \text{if } C(\mathbf{v}_{i-n+1}^{i}) > k \\ \alpha(\mathbf{v}_{i-n+1}^{i-1})\hat{P}_{bo}(v_i \mid \mathbf{v}_{i-n+2}^{i-1}) & \text{otherwise} \end{cases}$$

where $f(v_i \mid \mathbf{v}_{i-n+1}^{i-1})$ is a discounting function that reserves some probability mass for the unseen events and $\alpha(\mathbf{v}_{i-n+1}^{i-1})$ ensures that the model will be consistent.

Essentially, this function means that if the n-gram has been seen k or more times in training, the conditional probability of a word given its history is proportional to the maximum likelihood estimate of that n-gram. Otherwise, the conditional probability is equal to the back-off conditional probability of the $(n-1)$-gram. The value of k is usually chosen to be 0. However, empirical testing may find better values for k.

There are a lot of successful discount techniques as, for example, Good-Turing [Katz (1987)], Witten-Bell [Witten and Bell (1991)], or the linear and absolute discounting methods [Ney *et al.* (1994)]. In this work only the Kneser-Ney discount, presented on [Kneser and Ney (1995)], will be used.

In the Kneser-Ney discount, the discounted probability is computed by subtracting a constant D from the n-gram count. The main idea of Kneser-Ney is to use a modified probability estimate for lower order n-grams used for backoff. Specifically, the modified probability for a lower order n-gram is taken to be proportional to the number of unique words that precede it in the training data. We can define the discounted probability as:

$$f(v_i|\mathbf{v}_{i-n+1}^{i-1}) = \frac{C(\mathbf{v}_{i-n+1}^{i}) - D0}{C(\mathbf{v}_{i-n+1}^{i-1})} \quad \text{for highest order n-grams}$$

$$f(v_i) = \frac{n(*v_i) - D1}{n(**)} \quad \text{for lower order n-grams}$$

where $n(*v_i) = \{v_{i-1} : C(v_{i-1}v_i) > 0\}$ is the number of different words v_{i-1} that precede v_i in the training data and where $n(**) = \{(v_{i-1}, v_i) :$

$C(v_{i-1}v_i) > 0\} = \sum_{v_i} n(*v_i)$. $D0$ and $D1$ represent two different discounting constants, because the original kneser-Ney discounting uses one discounting constant for each n-gram order. These constants are estimated as:

$$D = \frac{n1}{(n1 + 2 \cdot n2)}$$

where $n1$ and $n2$ are the total number of n-grams with exactly one and two counts.

n-grams modelled by a stochastic finite state automaton

Along this work, stochastic finite state automata (SFSA) are often used to represent HMMs, lexical models and language models. Thanks to the homogeneous finite-state nature of all these models, they can be easily integrated into a single global finite state model. A n-gram can be represented using a SFSA [Vidal *et al.* (2005a,b)], defined as a sextuple $A = (Q, V, \delta, q_0, P, F)$, where:

- V is non-empty finite set of symbols
- $Q \subseteq V^{n-1} \cup q_0$ is a finite, not-empty set of states. Each state is defined using the vocabulary symbols V as $q = (v_{i-n+1}...v_{i-2}v_{i-1}) \in Q$
- $\delta \subset Q \times V \times Q$ is the state-transition function. A transition is denoted as:

$$(v_{i-n+1}...v_{i-2}v_{i-1}, v, v_{i-n+2}...v_{i-1}v)$$

  where $(v_{i-n+1}...v_{i-2}v_{i-1}) \in Q$, $(v_{i-n+2}...v_{i-1}v) \in Q$, and $v \in V$
- q_0 is the initial state $(q_0 \in Q)$
- $P : \delta \to \Re^+$ is the probability transition function. We are using deterministic SFSA, so each transition is identified with only the source state $q \in V^{n-1}$ and the transition symbol $v \in V$. Therefore, $P(q, v, q') = P(v|q)$
- $F : Q \to \Re^+$ is the final state probability function.

Figure 1.3 illustrates the use of SFSA to represent 1-gram, 2-grams and 3-grams.

In Fig. 1.4 we can see the example of a back-off smoothed n-gram using a SFSA.

1.3.3 *Interactive Pattern Recognition*

The idea of interaction between humans and machines is by no means new. In fact, historically, machines have mostly been developed with the aim of

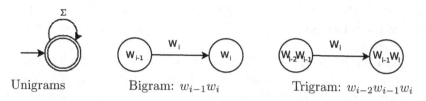

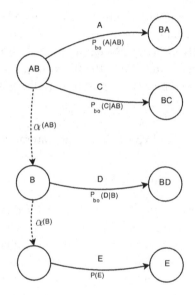

Fig. 1.3   Examples of *n*-grams represented using a SFSA.

Fig. 1.4   Examples of a SFSA representing a back-off smoothed *n*-gram.

assisting human beings in their work. Since the introduction of computer machinery, however, the idea of fully automatic devices that would completely substitute the humans in certain types of tasks, has been gaining increasing popularity. This is the case in areas such as PR. Scientific and technical research in this area have followed the "full automation" paradigm traditionally, even though, in practice, full automation often proves elusive or unnatural in many applications where technology is expected to *assist* rather than replace the human agents.

Placing PR within the human-interaction framework requires fundamental changes in the way we look at problems in this area. Interestingly, these changes entail important research opportunities which hold promise for a new generation of truly human-friendly PR devices. These opportunities are considered in [Vidal *et al.* (2007b); Toselli *et al.* (2011)], where tight interrelations between *user feedback*, *multimodality* and *adaptive learning* are examined.

The CATTI and MM-CATTI scenarios presented in this book (Chap. 4 and Chap. 5 respectively) study both the user feedback and the multimodality opportunities of this framework. However, adaptive learning is not considered here. Therefore, system operation is supposed to be driven by *fixed* statistical models.

In this subsection we review how human feedback can be directly used to improve the system performance and discuss the multimodal issues entailed by the resulting Interactive Pattern Recognition (IPR) framework.

In traditional PR [Duda and Hart (1973)], for a given input x, a best hypothesis is one which maximizes the posterior probability:

$$\hat{h} = \underset{h \in \mathcal{H}}{\operatorname{argmax}} \Pr(h \mid x) \tag{1.4}$$

where $\mathcal{H}$ is the set of possible hypotheses. Now, interaction allows adding more *conditions*:

$$\hat{h} = \underset{h \in \mathcal{H}}{\operatorname{argmax}} \Pr(h \mid x, f) \tag{1.5}$$

where $f \in F$ stands for the feedback, interaction-derived informations; e.g., in the form of *partial hypotheses* or *constraints* on $\mathcal{H}$. The new system hypothesis, $\hat{h}$, may prompt the user to provide further feedback informations, thereby starting a new interaction step. The process continues this way until the system output is acceptable by the user. Clearly, the richer the feedback signals f in (1.5) the greater the opportunity to obtain better $\hat{h}$. But solving the maximization (1.5) may be more difficult than in the case of our familiar $\Pr(h \mid x)$. Adequate solutions are discussed in the following chapters for HTR applications (see Chap. 4 and Chap. 5) .

In general, interactive processing makes history from previous interaction steps available. Taking jointly into account feedback and prediction history may significantly improve the prediction accuracy. Let h' be the history. It can be represented by the optimal hypothesis, $\hat{h}$, obtained by the system in its previous interaction step for the given x. Since previous hypotheses have been supervised/corrected by the user, a part of h' will be correct for the given x. In the current interaction step, the feedback f typically aims at (further) correcting elements of h'. Taking history into account, and applying the Bayes rule, Eq. 1.5 becomes:

$$\hat{h} = \underset{h \in \mathcal{H}}{\operatorname{argmax}} \Pr(h \mid x, h', f) = \underset{h \in \mathcal{H}}{\operatorname{argmax}} \Pr(x \mid h', f, h) \cdot \Pr(h \mid h', f) \tag{1.6}$$

It is worth noting that, by jointly considering the pair (h', f) as a kind of "consolidated history", this equation becomes formally identical to Eq. 1.5.

Using a deterministic feedback modality, such as keyboard or mouse, greatly simplify matters. Led D be the space of decoded feedback signals. Deterministic feedback decoding can then be specified as a function, $d :$ $F \to D$, which maps each raw feedback signal, f, into its corresponding unique decoding $d = d(f)$. For instance, if f is the signal of a keystroke on the key "A", $d(f)$ is the symbol "A" itself (keyboard are not expected to produce erroneous output symbols). Such determinism means that feedback signals do not need to be actually "decoded" and we can interchangeably use a feedback signal f and its unique decoding d. Therefore, using d rather than f in Eq. 1.6 we can now write:

$$\hat{h} = \underset{h \in \mathcal{H}}{\operatorname{argmax}} \Pr(h \mid x, h', d) = \underset{h \in \mathcal{H}}{\operatorname{argmax}} \Pr(x \mid h', d, h) \cdot \Pr(h \mid h', d) \quad (1.7)$$

It is interesting to note that, in general, the interaction feedback informations f do not naturally belong to the original domain from which the main data, x, come from. This observation is particularly interesting in the case of non-deterministic feedback. In this case, human interaction naturally entails some sort of *multimodality*. The challenge here is how to achieve and adequate modality synergy which finally allows taking maximum advantage of all the modalities involved.

Consider for instance that x is an image and f the acoustic signal of a speech command possibly describing (some of) the image contents. Since f is not deterministic, it has to be decoded. By considering the decoding of f, d, as a hidden variable in Eq. 1.6, we can write:

$$\hat{h} = \underset{h \in \mathcal{H}}{\operatorname{argmax}} \Pr(h \mid x, h', f) = \underset{h \in \mathcal{H}}{\operatorname{argmax}} \sum_{d} \Pr(h, d \mid x, h', f) \quad (1.8)$$

Approximating the sum with the dominating term, applying basic probability rules and ignoring terms which do not depend on the optimisation variables (h and d):

$$\hat{h} \approx \underset{h \in \mathcal{H}}{\operatorname{argmax}} \max_{d} \Pr(h \mid d, x, h', f) \cdot \Pr(d \mid h', x) \cdot \Pr(f \mid d, h', x) \quad (1.9)$$

Then, assuming independence of $\Pr(h \mid d, x, h', f)$ on f given h', d, x, of $\Pr(d \mid h', x)$ on x given h', of $\Pr(f \mid d, h', x)$ on h', x given d and applying the Bayes rule:

$$\hat{h} \approx \underset{h \in \mathcal{H}}{\operatorname{argmax}} \max_{d} \Pr(x \mid h', d, h) \cdot \Pr(h \mid d, h') \cdot \Pr(d \mid h') \cdot \Pr(f \mid d) \quad (1.10)$$

The first two terms of Eq. 1.10 are the same used in Eq. 1.7 for the basic IPR formulation with deterministic feedback. The other two terms are now needed to decode the non-deterministic user feedback. Interestingly, except for the history condition on the prior, these two terms are the same as those that would be needed to apply Eq. 1.4 of conventional PR for the recognition of feedback signals. But now we can condition the prior by the interaction history and, moreover, Eq 1.10 entails a joint optimisation for simultaneous recognition of main (x) and feedback (f) data. Obviously, this offers clear opportunities for more accurate feedback decoding than using just a conventional, off-the-shelf PR system for feedback signals recognition [Toselli *et al.* (2011)].

1.3.4   *Word-graphs*

As we will see in Chap. 4, a direct adaptation of the Viterbi algorithm to implement the CATTI system leads to a computational cost that grows quadratically with the number of words of each sentence. This can be problematic for large sentences and/or for fine-grained (character-level) interaction schemes. Word-graph techniques can be used to achieve very efficient, linear cost search. In this section basic word graph concepts are introduced.

A word graph (WG) is a data structure that represents a large finite sample of word sequences in a very efficient way. Formally, a WG is a weighted directed acyclic graph (WDAG) defined by the eight tuple $WG = (Q, n_I, F, V, A, t, p, \omega)$:

- Q is a finite set of nodes. Since a WG is a DAG, a topological order of the nodes is assumed and each node n is labelled with its corresponding index in this order: $Q = \{0, 1, ..., |Q| - 1\}$.
- $n_I \in Q$ is an initial node: $n_I = 0$.
- $F \subseteq Q$ is a set of final nodes.
- V is a non-empty set of words (vocabulary).
- $A \subset Q \times Q$ is a finite set of edges. Each edge e is denoted by its departing and ending nodes: $e = (i, j)$ where $i, j \in Q$, and $i < j$.
- $t : Q \rightarrow \{0, 1, ...T\}$ is a position function that associates each node (except n_I) with a position of the input vector sequence $\mathbf{x} = \mathbf{x}_1^T$ (that is, with a horizontal position of the input handwritten image). It must comply: $t(n_I) = 0$ and $\forall_{n \in F} \ t(n) = T$.
- $\omega : A \rightarrow V$ is a function that associates a word to each edge. Given

the edge $e = (i, j)$, $\omega(e)$ is a word hypothesis between horizontal image positions $t(i) + 1$ and $t(j)$.

- $p : A \rightarrow [0, 1]$ is an edge probability function. Typically, given an edge $e = (i, j)$, $p(e)$ is a probability or score assigned to the hypothesis that $\omega(e)$ appears between $t(i) + 1$ and $t(j)$.

An illustrative example of a word graph is shown in Fig. 1.5. This word graph represents a set of possible transcriptions of a handwritten line image containing the text "*only one among thousands who do not*".

Formally, a path in a WG is a sequence of consecutive edges $\phi = \{e_1 = (z_0, z_1), e_2 = (z_1, z_2), ..., e_l = (z_{l-1}, z_l)\}$ of the WG, where $z_k \in Q$ and $0 \leq k \leq l$. We say that a path is complete if $z_0 = n_I$ and $z_l \in F$. The probability of a path is computed as the product of the probabilities of the edges along the path:

$$P(\phi) = \prod_{i=1}^{l} p(e_i) \tag{1.11}$$

The word subsequence associated to this path is $\mathbf{w} = \omega(e_1)\omega(e_2)...\omega(e_l)$. Given that WGs are generally ambiguous (for each node and word there may be several possible next nodes), in general there is more than one path that accounts for the sequence $\mathbf{w}$. Let $\sigma(\mathbf{w})$ be the set of all these paths and let $\phi_{\mathbf{w}}$ be one of these paths, the probability of the word subsequence $\mathbf{w}$ is computed as:

$$P(\mathbf{w}) = \sum_{\phi_{\mathbf{w}} \in \sigma(\mathbf{w})} P(\phi_{\mathbf{w}}) \tag{1.12}$$

The word graphs are used here as a efficient representation of transcription hypotheses of a handwritten text image. These word sequence hypotheses are formed by the concatenation of words of complete paths; that is, paths from the initial node to a final node in the WG. Therefore, the probability of a complete word sequence is analogous to the previous one, but considering only the set of complete paths, $\int(\mathbf{w})$, associated with $\mathbf{w}$:

$$P(\mathbf{w}) = \sum_{\phi_{\mathbf{w}} \in \int(\mathbf{w})} P(\phi_{\mathbf{w}}) \tag{1.13}$$

Given a WG, the complete word sequence, $\mathbf{w}$, with greatest probability is:

$$\hat{\mathbf{w}} = \underset{\mathbf{w}}{\operatorname{argmax}} \sum_{\phi_{\mathbf{w}} \in \int(\mathbf{w})} P(\phi_{\mathbf{w}}) \tag{1.14}$$

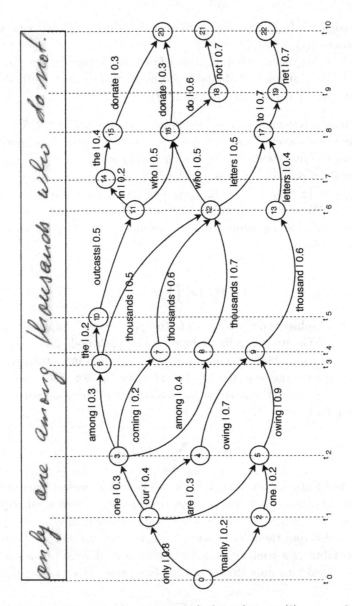

Fig. 1.5   Image positions t_i are associates with the nodes as: $t(0) = t_0 = 0$, $t(1) = t(2) = t_1$, $t(3) = t(4) = t(5) = t_2$, $t(6) = t_3$, $t(7) = t(8) = t(9) = t_4$, $t(10) = t_5$, $t(11) = t(12) = t(13) = t_6$, $t(14) = t_7$, $t(15) = t(16) = t(17) = t_8$, $t(18) = t(19) = t_9$, $t(20) = t(21) = t(22) = t_{10}$.

It should be noted that the maximization problem stated in Eq. (1.14) is NP-hard [Casacuberta and de la Higuera (2000)]. Nevertheless, adequate approximations can be obtained by using only the dominant term of the sum:

$$P(\mathbf{w}) \approx P(\tilde{\mathbf{w}}) = \max_{\phi_{\mathbf{w}} \in f(\mathbf{w})} P(\phi_{\mathbf{w}}) \qquad (1.15)$$

which can be solved by means of efficient search algorithms, like Viterbi [Jelinek (1998)]. This maximization provides $\tilde{\mathbf{w}}$, that is, the sequence of words associated to the best path.

For example, given the WG represented in Fig. 1.5, the probability of the path ϕ_5:

$$\phi_5 = \{(0,1), (1,3), (3,6), (6,12), (12,16), (16,18), (18,21)\}$$

is computed as:

$$P(\phi_5) = p(0,1)p(1,3)p(3,6)p(6,12)p(12,16)p(16,18)p(18,21)$$
$$= 0.8 \cdot 0.3 \cdot 0.3 \cdot 0.5 \cdot 0.5 \cdot 0.6 \cdot 0.7 = 0.0076$$

The word sequence associated with this path is the correct transcription of the sentence, $\mathbf{w}_4$=*"only one among thousands who do not"*. However, ϕ_5 is not the only path that generates $\mathbf{w}_4$,

$$\phi_6 = \{(0,1), (1,3), (3,8), (8,12), (12,16), (16,18), (18,21)\}$$

generates it too. So, the exact probability of $\mathbf{w}_4$ is:

$$P(\mathbf{w}_4) = P(\phi_5) + P(\phi_6) = 0.0076 + 0.0141 = 0.0217$$

and using the Viterbi approximation, the probability of $\mathbf{w}_4$ is the probability of the path with maximum probability, i.e:

$$P(\mathbf{w}_4) \approx P(\tilde{\mathbf{w}}_4) = P(\phi_6) = 0.0141$$

Now, to obtain the word sequence with greater probability all the word sequences on the WG must be taken into account. Next, we can see all the word sequences in the WG of Fig. 1.5 and their corresponding paths and probabilities:

- $\mathbf{w}_1$=*"only our owing thousand letters to net"*
  $\phi_1 = \{(0,1), (1,4), (4,9), (9,13), (13,17), (17,19), (19,22)\}$
  $P(\mathbf{w}_1) = P(\phi_1) = 0.0263$

- $\mathbf{w}_2$="*only are owing thousand letters to net*"
  $\phi_2 = \{(0,1),(1,5),(5,9),(9,13),(13,17),(17,19),(19,22)\}$
  $P(\mathbf{w}_2) = P(\phi_2) = 0.0254$

- $\mathbf{w}_3$="*only one among thousands letters to net*"
  $\phi_3 = \{(0,1),(1,3),(3,6),(6,12),(12,17),(17,19),(19,22)\}$
  $\phi_4 = \{(0,1),(1,3),(3,8),(8,12),(12,17),(17,19),(19,22)\}$
  $P(\mathbf{w}_3) = P(\phi_3) + P(\phi_4) = 0.0088 + 0.0164 = 0.0252$

- $\mathbf{w}_4$="*only one among thousands who do not*"
  $\phi_5 = \{(0,1),(1,3),(3,6),(6,12),(12,16),(16,18),(18,21)\}$
  $\phi_6 = \{(0,1),(1,3),(3,8),(8,12),(12,16),(16,18),(18,21)\}$
  $P(\mathbf{w}_4) = P(\phi_5) + P(\phi_6) = 0.0076 + 0.0141 = 0.0217$

- $\mathbf{w}_5$="*only one among thousands who donate*"
  $\phi_7 = \{(0,1),(1,3),(3,6),(6,12),(12,16),(16,20)\}$
  $\phi_8 = \{(0,1),(1,3),(3,8),(8,12),(12,16),(16,20)\}$
  $P(\mathbf{w}_5) = P(\phi_7) + P(\phi_8) = 0.0054 + 0.0100 = 0.0154$

- $\mathbf{w}_6$="*only one coming thousands who donate*"
  $\phi_9 = \{(0,1),(1,3),(3,7),(7,12),(12,16),(16,20)\}$
  $P(\mathbf{w}_6) = P(\phi_9) = 0.0043$

- $\mathbf{w}_7$="*mainly one owing thousand letters to net*"
  $\phi_{10} = \{(0,2),(2,5),(5,9),(9,13),(13,17),(17,19),(19,22)\}$
  $P(\mathbf{w}_7) = P(\phi_{10}) = 0.0042$

- $\mathbf{w}_8$="*only one among the outcasts who do not*"
  $\phi_{11} = \{(0,1),(1,3),(3,6),(6,10),(10,11),(11,16),(16,18),(18,21)\}$
  $P(\mathbf{w}_8) = P(\phi_1 1) = 0.0015$

- $\mathbf{w}_9$="*only one among the outcasts who donate*"
  $\phi_{12} = \{(0,1),(1,3),(3,6),(6,10),(10,11),(11,16),(16,20)\}$
  $P(\mathbf{w}_9) = P(\phi_{12}) = 0.0010$

- $\mathbf{w}_{10}$="*only one coming thousands letters to net*"
  $\phi_{13} = \{(0,1),(1,3),(3,7),(7,12),(12,17),(17,19),(19,22)\}$
  $P(\mathbf{w}_{10}) = P(\phi_{13}) = 0.007$

- $\mathbf{w}_{11}$=*"only one coming thousands who do not"*
  $\phi_{14} = \{(0,1),(1,3),(3,7),(7,12),(12,16),(16,18),(18,21)\}$
  $P(\mathbf{w}_{11}) = P(\phi_{14}) = 0.006$

- $\mathbf{w}_{12}$=*"only one among the outcasts in the donate"*
  $\phi_{15} = \{(0,1),(1,3),(3,6),(6,10),(10,11),(11,14),(14,15),(15,20)\}$
  $P(\mathbf{w}_{11}) = P(\phi_{15}) = 0.0002$

So, the word sequence with greater probability is $\mathbf{w}_1$ for both exact probabilities and probabilities approximated using the Viterbi algorithm $(P(\mathbf{w}_1) = P(\tilde{\mathbf{w}}_1) = 0.0263)$.

Sometimes, it can be necessary not only to compute the best word sequence, but also the n-best word sequences in the word graph. To this end, the algorithm known as "Recursive Enumeration Algorithm" (REA) [Jiménez and marzal (1999)] can be advantageously used for its simplicity to calculate best paths on demand.

1.4 Assessing Computer Assisted Transcription of Handwritten Text Images

In the framework of interactive transcription of handwritten text images, a human expert is embedded in the transcription process. So, the system performance has to be assessed mainly in terms of how much human effort is required to achieve the perfect transcription of the handwritten text images.

However, evaluating system performance in this scenario should require prohibitively expensive and time consuming human work and judgement. In order to assess the validity of our assumptions and estimations, it will not be enough with just one transcriber expert, but an entire panel of transcribers will be required. Each one of these transcribers ought to carry out several trials, where each trial round should include at least one dry-run session, during which the participant is asked to transcribe some document using the same interface but without the benefit of the system's predictions. And it must be taken into account that, using the same document to transcribe in both sessions would be unfair, because the user would tend to familiarize herself with the text during the dry-run session, thereby apparently achieving much higher productivity in the second session. However, if different texts are used the results will not be comparable. Consequently, a better solution might be to work with the same document but allowing a lot of time to pass between experiments. In addition, for these experiments to lead to reliable results, appropriate interfaces for professional use must be implemented. This kind of experiments were carried out in the TT2 project [SchlumbergerSema S.A. *et al.* (2002-2005)] in which interactive-predictive approaches were developed and tested for hight-quality Computer-Assisted Translation. While corpus-based, objective effort reduction measures did provide useful research feedback information [Barrachina *et al.* (2009)], only rather vague, mostly qualitative conclusions could be finally derived from the (otherwise extremely expensive) experiments with real users [Casacuberta *et al.* (2009)].

Fortunately, the very convenient and successful PR assessment paradigm based on labelled corpora is still applicable in many IPR cases to obtain adequate *estimates* of human effort required to achieve the goals of the considered tasks.

A corpus designed for testing a traditional, non-interactive HTR system consists of a collection of handwritten text lines, each one accompanied by its corresponding perfect transcription. Performance is computed in terms of word/character errors; i.e., by counting the number of words/character from the system hypothesis transcription that differ from the corresponding correct word/character. Although in the interactive scenario the importance of the recognition errors is diminished (as the user will ensure that no errors will be produced), the correct labelling for each text line image can be used to determine how many interaction steps are needed to produce a correct hypothesis.

In the case of interactive transcription systems, the effort needed by a human transcriber to produce correct transcriptions is estimated by the *Word Stroke Ratio* (WSR) and the *Key Stroke Ratio* (KSR), depending if the interactions are carried out at word or at character level (see Chap. 4). These measures are computed using the reference transcriptions. After each recognition hypothesis, the longest common prefix between the hypothesis and the reference is obtained and the first unmatching word/character from the hypothesis is replaced by the corresponding reference word/character. This process is iterated until a full match with the reference is achieved. Therefore, the WSR/KSR can be defined as the number of (word/character level) user interactions that are necessary to achieve the reference transcription of the text image considered, divided by the total number of reference words/characters.

Chapter 2

Corpora

2.1 Introduction

In this chapter, the main features of the different corpora used in the empirical tests presented throughout this book are exposed. Each of these corpora encompasses both the text images and the corresponding transcriptions of these images. Transcriptions are needed both in the training data, to train the HTR models, and in the test data, to assess the performance of the trained models.

We have used four different corpora. Three of them correspond to off-line handwritten text images, and the last one is an on-line handwritten text corpus. The first off-line corpus was compiled from an historic handwritten document identified as "Cristo-Salvador" (CS). The second one, called ODEC, consists of handwritten answers from survey forms. The last off-line corpus, called IAMDB, consists of handwritten full English sentences based on the Lancaster-Oslo/Bergen (LOB) corpus. On the other hand, the on-line corpus, called UNIPEN, is an English dataset divided into several categories: letters, digits, symbols, isolated words and full sentences.

2.2 CS

The corpus was compiled from a document from the XIX century, handwritten in Spanish by a single writer. It was kindly provided by the *Biblioteca Valenciana Digital* (BIVALDI)[1] in the form of page images scanned at 300 dpi.

It is a legacy document which suffers the typical degradation problems

---

[1] http://bv2.gva.es

Fig. 2.1   Examples of the CS corpus.

of this kind of documents [Drida (2006)]. Among these are the presence of smear, significant background variations and uneven illumination, spots due to the humidity, and marks resulting from the ink that goes through the paper (generally called bleed-through). In addition, other kind of difficulties appear in these pages as different sizes in the words, underlined and crossed-out words, etc. The combination of these problems increase the recognition difficulty.

CS is a rather small document composed of 53 colour images of text pages. Some of these page images are shown in the Fig. 2.1 and Fig. 2.2 shows a detailed portion of one of these pages.

The page images were preprocessed and automatically divided into lines (see Sec. 3.2.1). The results were visually inspected and the few line-separation errors (around 4%) were manually corrected, resulting in a data-set of 1,172 text line images. The transcriptions corresponding to line images are also available, containing 10,918 running words with a vocabulary of 3,287 different words.

Two different partitions were defined for this data-set. In the first one, called *page* (or *soft*), the test set is formed by 491 line samples corresponding to the last ten lines of each document page, whereas the training set is composed of the 681 remaining lines. On the other hand, in the second partition, called *book* (or *hard*), the test set is composed of 497 line samples

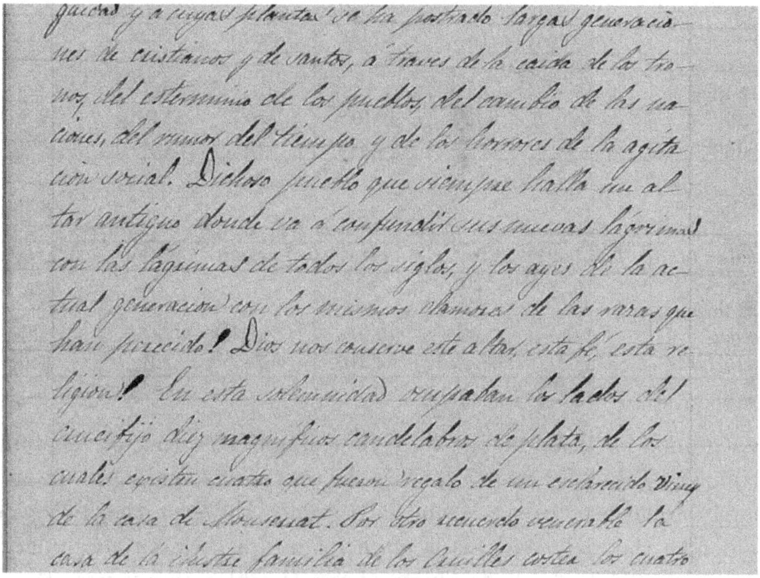

gueros y a cuyas plantas se ha postrado largas generacio-
nes de cristianos y de santos, a través de la caida de los tro-
nos, del exterminio de los pueblos, del cambio de las na-
ciones, del rumor del tiempo y de los horrores de la agita-
cion social. Dichoso pueblo que siempre halla su altar antiguo donde va a confundir sus nuevas lágrimas
con las lágrimas de todos los siglos, y los ayes de la actual generacion con los mismos clamores de las razas que
han perecido! Dios nos conserve este altar, esta fe, esta religion! En esta solemnidad ocupaban los lados del
crucifijo diez magnificos candelabros de plata, de los
cuales existen cuatro que fueron regalo de un esclarecido Virey
de la casa de Monserrat. Por otro recuerdo venerable la
casa de la ilustre familia de los Cruilles costea los cuatro

Fig. 2.2 Detailed section of a page from the CS corpus.

belonging to the last 20 document pages, whereas the remaining 675 lines (the 33 initial pages) were assigned to the training set.

Note that, the *page* partition is considered to be easier to recognize than the *book* one because its test line samples were extracted from the same pages as the training text line samples. On the other hand, the *book* partition better approaches a realistic transcription process. That is, the system is initially trained with the first document pages, and then as more page images are transcribed, a greater amount of samples (line images and transcriptions) become available to retrain the system and thereby improve the transcription of the rest of the document.

To train the HMMs, all the elements (including capital letters, punctuation marks, etc.) appearing in each handwritten text image of the training set are distinguished. However, to train the n-gram models, uppercase characters are converted to lowercase and the punctuation marks and diacritics are eliminated. The simplified transcriptions of the training set are used to train the language models and those of the test set are used as references to assess performance. All the information related with *page* and *book* partitions is summarized in the Tables 2.1 and 2.2 respectively.

The number of different words of the test partition that do not appear

Table 2.1 Basic statistics of the partition *page* of the CS database.

Number of:	Training	Test	Total	Lexicon	OOV	Tr. Ratio
Pages	53	53	53	–	–	–
Text lines	681	491	1,172	–	–	–
Words	6,435	4,483	10,918	2,277	1,010	2.8
Characters	36,729	25,487	62,216	78	0	470

Table 2.2 Basic statistics of the partition *book* of the CS database.

Number of:	Training	Test	Total	Lexicon	OOV	Tr. Ratio
Pages	33	20	53	–	–	–
Text lines	675	497	1,172	–	–	–
Words	6,227	4,691	10,918	2,237	1,050	2.8
Characters	35,863	26,353	62,216	78	0	460

in the training partition is shown in the column OOV (out of vocabulary words) in the Tables 2.1 and 2.2. Only the text corresponding to the training partition has been used to train the n-grams. However, the OOV words are added to the lexicon. This is often referred as "closed vocabulary"[2]. On the other hand, the last column shows the *"training ratio"*, that is, the average number of times that one word/character has appeared in the training text.

It is important to remark that both partitions of this corpus have quite a small training ratio (around 2.8 training running words per lexicon-entry). Moreover, the closed-vocabulary test-set perplexity computed with a bigram language model trained on the training text is about 360 in the book partition. The small training ratio, along with the large perplexity, are expected to result in undertrained (n-gram) language models, which will clearly increase the difficulty of the prediction.

This corpus is publicly available at http://prhlt.iti.es.

2.3 ODEC

This corpus consists of casual, spontaneous handwriting phrase images [Toselli (2004); Toselli *et al.* (2004b)]. It was compiled from handwritten answers in Spanish, extracted from survey forms made for a telecommunication company[3].

---

[2]Such as "closed vocabulary" scheme is commonly used in automatic speech recognition [Jelinek (1998)] to ease results reproducibility.
[3]Data kindly provided by ODEC S.A. (www.odec.es)

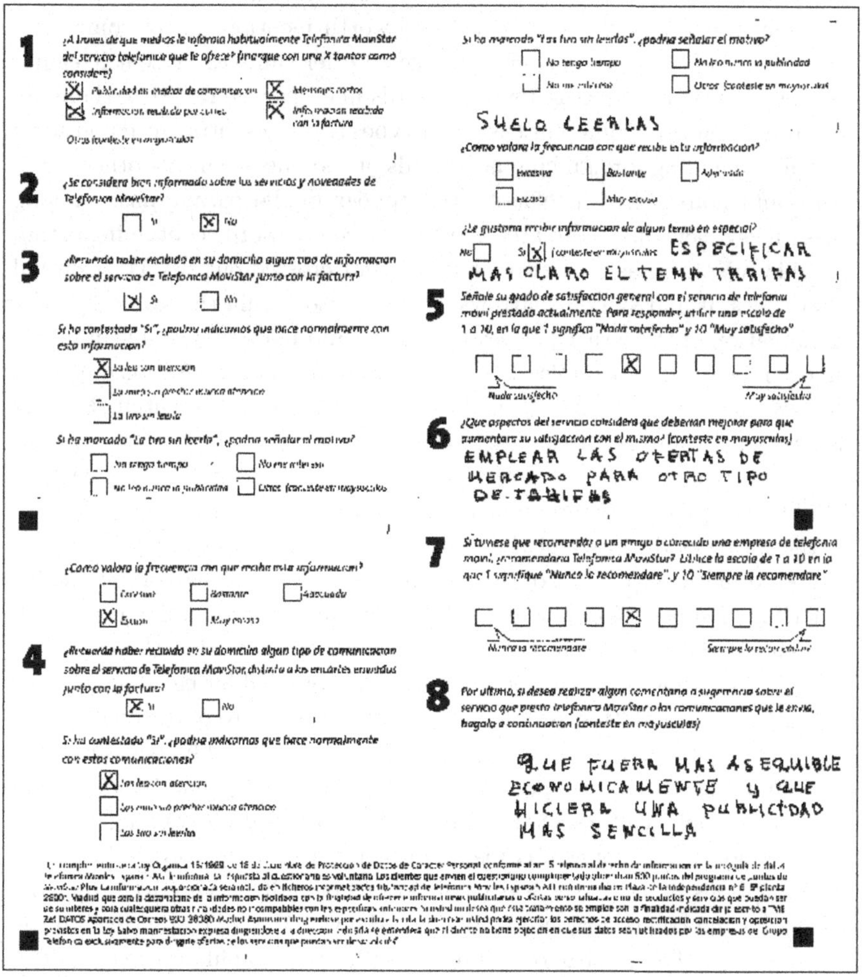

1 ¿A través de qué medios le informa habitualmente Telefónica MoviStar del servicio telefónico que le ofrece? (marque con una X tantos como considere)

[X] Publicidad en medios de comunicación [X] Mensajes cortos
[X] Información recibida por correo [X] Información recibida con la factura

2 ¿Se considera bien informado sobre los servicios y novedades de Telefónica MoviStar?

[ ] Sí [X] No

3 ¿Recuerda haber recibido en su domicilio algún tipo de información sobre el servicio de Telefónica MoviStar junto con la factura?

[X] Sí [ ] No

Si ha contestado "Sí", ¿podría indicarnos qué hace normalmente con esta información?

[X] Se lee con atención
[ ] La miro y no presto mucha atención
[ ] La tiro sin leerla

Si ha marcado "La tiro sin leerla", ¿podría señalar el motivo?

[ ] No tengo tiempo [ ] No me interesa
[ ] No leo nunca la publicidad [ ] Otros (conteste en mayúsculas)

¿Cómo valora la frecuencia con que recibe esta información?

[ ] Excesiva [ ] Bastante [ ] Adecuada
[X] Escasa [ ] Muy escasa

4 ¿Recuerda haber recibido en su domicilio algún tipo de comunicación sobre el servicio de Telefónica MoviStar, distinta a los enviados junto con la factura?

[X] Sí [ ] No

Si ha contestado "Sí", ¿podría indicarnos qué hace normalmente con estas comunicaciones?

[X] Las leo con atención
[ ] Las miro y no presto mucha atención
[ ] Las tiro sin leerlas

Si ha marcado "Las tiro sin leerlas", ¿podría señalar el motivo?

[ ] No tengo tiempo [ ] No leo nunca la publicidad
[ ] No me interesa [ ] Otros (conteste en mayúsculas)

SUELO LEERLAS

¿Cómo valora la frecuencia con que recibe esta información?

[ ] Excesiva [ ] Bastante [ ] Adecuada
[ ] Escasa [ ] Muy escasa

¿Le gustaría recibir información de algún tema en especial?

No [ ] Sí [X] (conteste en mayúsculas) ESPECIFICAR MAS CLARO EL TEMA TARIFAS

5 Señale su grado de satisfacción general con el servicio de telefonía móvil prestado actualmente. Para responder, utilice una escala de 1 a 10, en la que 1 significa "Nada satisfecho" y 10 "Muy satisfecho"

Nada satisfecho [ ] [ ] [ ] [ ] [X] [ ] [ ] [ ] [ ] [ ] Muy satisfecho

6 ¿Qué aspectos del servicio considera que deberían mejorar para que aumentara su satisfacción con el mismo? (conteste en mayúsculas)

EMPLEAR LAS OFERTAS DE MERCADO PARA OTRO TIPO DE TARIFAS

7 Si tuviese que recomendar a un amigo o conocido una empresa de telefonía móvil, ¿recomendaría Telefónica MoviStar? Utilice la escala de 1 a 10 en la que 1 signifique "Nunca la recomendaré", y 10 "Siempre la recomendaré"

Nunca la recomendaré [ ] [ ] [ ] [ ] [X] [ ] [ ] [ ] [ ] [ ] Siempre la recomendaré

8 Por último, si desea realizar algún comentario o sugerencia sobre el servicio que presta Telefónica MoviStar o las comunicaciones que le envía, hágalo a continuación (conteste en mayúsculas)

QUE FUERA MAS ASEQUIBLE ECONOMICAMENTE Y QUE HICIERA UNA PUBLICIDAD MAS SENCILLA

Fig. 2.3 A sample form from the ODEC Database.

The handwritten sentences are answers in the "suggestions" field of the forms (see Fig. 2.3, point 8). These answers were written by a heterogeneous group of people, without any explicit or formal restriction. In addition, since no guidelines were given as to the kind of pen or the writing style to be used, paragraphs become very variable and noisy. Some of the difficulties involved in this task are worth mentioning. In some samples, the stroke thickness is non-uniform. Other samples present irregular and non-consistent spacing between words and characters. Also, there are words written using different case, font types and sizes intra-word and some samples including foreign language words or sentences. On the other hand, noise and non-textual artefacts often appear in the paragraphs. Among these noisy elements there are unknown words or words containing orthographic mistakes, as well as underlined and crossed-out words. Unusual abbreviations and symbols, arrows, etc. are also within this category. The combination of the writing-styles variability and noise may result in partly or entirely illegible samples and make preprocessing operations such as deskew, deslanting, or size normalization (see Chap. 3), essential. Fig. 2.4 shows some examples of this variability.

The image data-set extracted from the ODEC survey forms consists of 913 binary images of handwritten paragraphs scanned at 300 dpi. Because of the inherent difficulty of the task, line extraction was carried out in a semi-automatic way. Most of the paragraphs were processed automatically, but manual supervision was applied to difficult line-overlapping cases such as some of those shown in Fig. 2.4. By adequately pasting the extracted lines, a single-line (long) image per form was obtained for each sample (see Fig. 2.5). The resulting set of sentences was randomly partitioned into a training set of 676 images and a test set of 237 images. The transcriptions corresponding to the images are also available, containing $16,371$ words with a vocabulary of $2,118$ different words. For n-gram training, the average ratio of running words instances per vocabulary word is 5.7. The transcriptions of sentences was carried out manually, trying to obtain the most detailed transcription possible. So, the words were transcribed in the same way as they appear on the text, with orthographic mistakes, alternating lowercase with uppercase, in the original language, etc. Some codes were defined to label the different artefacts that appear on the text, such as signs, crossed-out words, arrows, etc. As in the CS corpora, to train the HMMs we consider all the elements appearing in the training text images. On the other hand, to train the n-gram models, uppercase characters are converted to lowercase, punctuation marks are eliminated, orthographic

Fig. 2.4 Examples of the answers in the "suggestion" field in the ODEC forms. In these examples we can see the differences on the stroke thickness, the irregular and non-consistent spacing between words and characters, the differences on the types and sizes of the words, words containing orthographic mistakes, crossed-out words, non-textual artefacts, etc.

mistakes are corrected and abbreviations are replaced with their full text equivalents [Toselli *et al.* (2004b)]. The bi-gram test-set perplexity is 199. More information can be found in Table 2.3.

Table 2.3 Basic statistics of the database ODEC.

Number of:	Training	Test	Total	Lexicon	OOV	Tr. Ratio
Phrases	676	237	913	–	–	–
Words	10,994	3,465	14,459	1,923	195	5.7
Characters	64,666	21,533	86,199	80	0	808

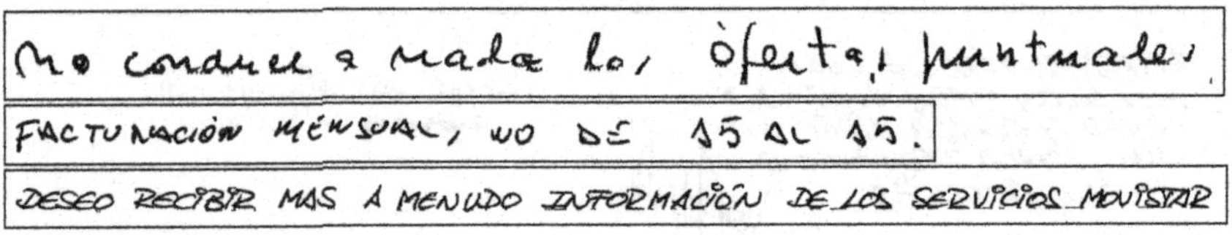

Fig. 2.5   Three (short) sample sentences from the ODEC Database after adequately pasting the extracted lines.

2.4   IAMDB

This corpus was compiled by the Research Group on Computer Vision and Artificial Intelligence (FKI) at the Institute of Computer Science an Applied Mathematics (IAM) in Bern (Switzerland). The database was first published in the ICDAR (International Conference of Document Analysis and Recognition) in 1999 [Marti and Bunke (1999)]. In the second version of the database, sentence and word segmentation schemes were used, as documented in [Zimmermann and Bunke (2000)]. The IAM-database as of October 2002 is described in [Marti and Bunke (2002)]. It is publicly accessible and freely available upon request for non-commercial research purposes (www.iam.unibe.ch/fki/databases/iam-handwriting-database). The IAMDB images correspond to handwritten texts copied from the Lancaster-Oslo/Bergen (LOB) corpus [Garsid *et al.* (1995); Johansson *et al.* (1978)], which encompasses around 500 printed electronic English texts of about 2,000 words each and about one million total running words.

The text in the LOB corpus is of quite diverse nature, composed of different categories (editorial, reportage, religion, skills, hobbies, science fiction, ...). The LOB corpus (see [Johansson *et al.* (1978)]) was compiled by researchers form Lancaster, Oslo and Bergen between 1970 and 1978. The text in the corpus was split into fragments of about 3 to 6 sentences with at least 50 words each. These text fragments were printed onto forms and different persons were asked to handwritten the text on one or more of these forms by hand. No restriction was imposed on the writing style or the type of pen to be used. The forms of unconstrained handwritten text were scanned at a resolution of 300dpi and saved as PNG images with 256 gray levels. Fig. 2.6 shows one of these forms.

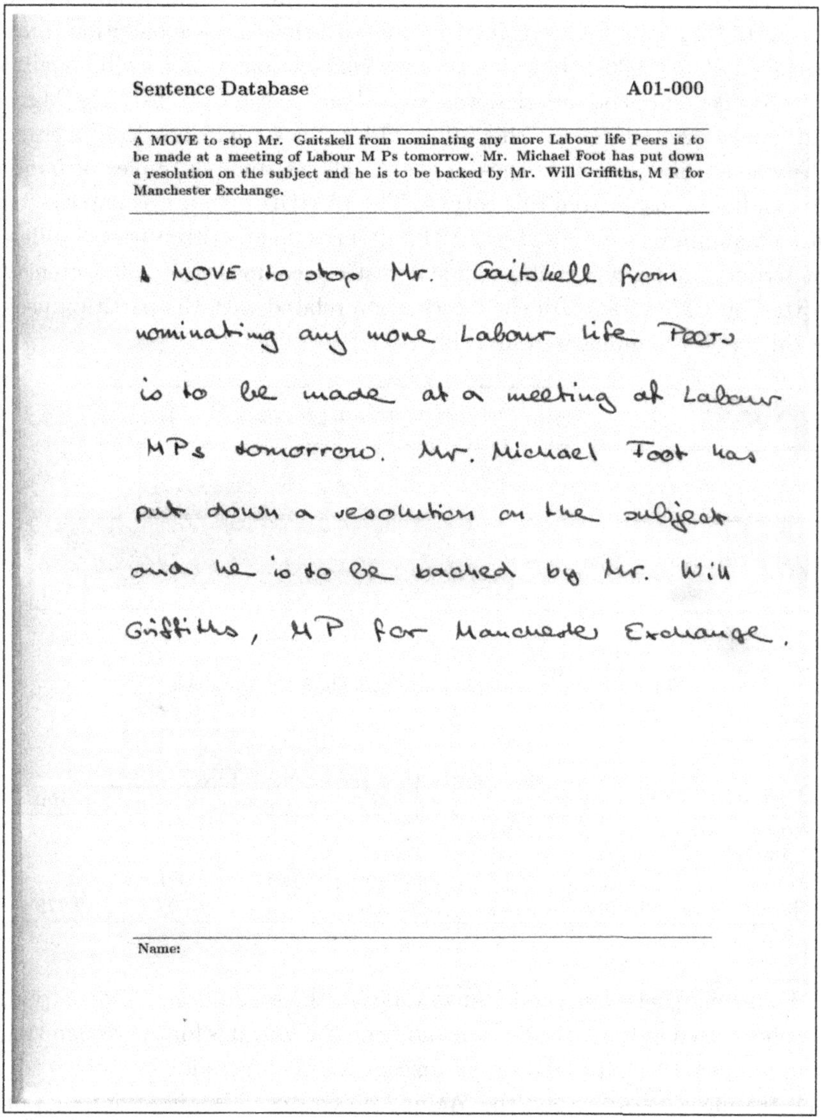

Sentence Database A01-000

A MOVE to stop Mr. Gaitskell from nominating any more Labour life Peers is to be made at a meeting of Labour M Ps tomorrow. Mr. Michael Foot has put down a resolution on the subject and he is to be backed by Mr. Will Griffiths, M P for Manchester Exchange.

A MOVE to stop Mr. Gaitskell from nominating any more Labour life Peers is to be made at a meeting of Labour MPs tomorrow. Mr. Michael Foot has put down a resolution on the subject and he is to be backed by Mr. Will Griffiths, MP for Manchester Exchange.

Name:

Fig. 2.6 A sample form from the IAM Database.

The IAMDB version 3.0 (the latest at this moment) is composed of 1,539 scanned text pages, handwritten by 657 different writers. This dataset is provided at different segmentation levels: sentences, lines and isolated words. In this book we are going to work with the sentence partition [Zimmermann *et al.* (2006)]. Line detection and extraction, as well as (manually) detecting sentences boundaries, was carried out by the IAM institute [Marti and Bunke (2001)]. Using this information, lines could be easily merged into whole sentence line-images. Fig. 2.7 shows some examples of handwritten lines images from this corpus. The IAMDB corpus was partitioned into a training set composed of 2,124 sentences, handwritten by 448 different writers, and a writer independent test set composed of 200 sentences written by 100 writers. All the information related with the partition used on this book is summarized in Table 2.4.

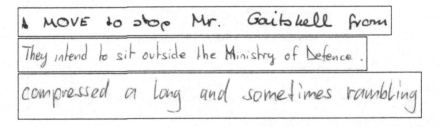

Fig. 2.7   Some sample lines from the IAM Database.

Table 2.4   Basic statistics of the database IAM.

Number of:	Training	Test	Total	Lexicon	OOV	Tr. Ratio
Writers	448	100	548	–	–	–
Sentences	2,124	200	2,324	–	–	–
Words	42,832	3,957	46,789	8,017	921	73
Characters	216,774	20,726	237,500	78	0	2,779

Following [Bertolami and Bunke (2008)], three additional text corpora have been used to build the lexicon and train the n-grams for the recognition task; namely, the full LOB corpus (except the sentences for the image test set), the Brown corpus and the Wellington corpus. Therefore, for n-gram training we have a quite good effective average ratio of 73 word instances per IAMDB vocabulary word. In this case, the bi-gram test-set perplexity is 370.

The Brown corpus was published by Francis and Kucera in 1964 [Francis and Kucera (1964)]. It was the first modern computer readable corpus and it corresponds to the LOB corpus in size and content, but contains words in American English.

The third corpus, which also equals the LOB corpus in size and content is the Wellington corpus [Holmes *et al.* (1998)], it contains words in New Zealand English.

Table 2.5 gives more information of the three text corpora.

Table 2.5 Description of the text corpora.

Number of:	LOB	Brown	Wellington
Lines	52,676	49,362	56,745
Running words	1,119,904	1,045,213	1,144,401
Vocabulary size	52,724	53,115	58,919
Running Characters	5,803,916	5,582,023	6,055,820

2.5 UNIPEN

The UNIPEN `Train-R01/V07` dataset is a publicly available English on-line HTR corpus[4]. It comes organized into several categories [Guyon *et al.* (1994)] such as lower and upper-case letters, digits, symbols, isolated words and full sentences. According to the UNIPEN categorization, the isolated digits category is identified as `1a`, isolated lowercase letters as `1c` and isolated symbols category as `1d`. Some character examples from these categories are shown in Fig. 2.8.

This corpus is used here to test the e-pen feedback in the MM-CATTI system described in Chap. 5. Unfortunately, the UNIPEN isolated words category does not contain all (or almost none of) the required word instances to be handwritten by the user in the MM-CATTI interaction process with the ODEC, IAMDB, or CS text images. Therefore, the needed on-line handwritten words were generated by concatenating random character instances from the three UNIPEN categories mentioned above: `1a` (digits), `1c` (lowercase letters) and `1d` (symbols). See Chap. 5 for details about this process. Table 2.6 shows basic statistics of these categories of the UNIPEN dataset and the corresponding partition definitions.

---

[4]For a detailed description of this dataset, see http://www.unipen.org.

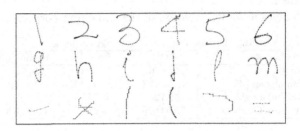

Fig. 2.8   Some examples from the categories 1a,1c and 1d in the Train-R01/V07 dataset.

Table 2.6   Basic statistics of the UNIPEN categories 1a,1c and 1d in the Train-R01/V07 dataset and their corresponding partition definitions.

Number of:	Train	Test	Total	lexicon
digits (1a)	9,032	6,921	15,953	10
letters (1c)	39,354	18,894	58,248	26
symbols (1d)	10,321	6,849	17,170	32
All Together	58,707	32,664	91,371	68

Chapter 3

Handwritten Text Recognition

WITH CONTRIBUTION OF: Moisés Pastor

3.1 Introduction

Handwritten text recognition (HTR) is not an easy task. The difficulties to segment text lines, the variability of the handwriting, the complexity of the styles and the open vocabulary make that the HTR systems do not obtain acceptable accuracy for unconstrained handwritten documents. However, human beings do carry out this process both accurately effortlessly in a natural way. Observing the way in which the humans do this recognition, it seems clear that such human ability is due to the inter-cooperation between different levels of knowledge. Perhaps the most important of these levels are: morphological, lexical and syntactic.

The situation in automatic speech recognition (ASR) is very similar [Jelinek (1998)]. So, it is natural that both ASR and HTR be tackled with techniques based on the cooperation of all the aforementioned knowledge sources [Bozinovic and Srihari (1989); El-Yacoubi *et al.* (1999); Senior and Robinson (1998); Plamondon and Srihari (2000); Marti and Bunke (2001)]. The different knowledge levels can be modelled using finite state models, such as HMMs, grammars or automata.

As mentioned in Chap. 1, depending on the mode of data acquisition used, automatic handwriting recognition can be classified into on-line and off-line. In this book, the input are images of handwritten text. Therefore, the main system (see Chap. 4) is an *off-line* HTR system. However, the feedback provided by the user in computer assisted HTR may come in the form of *on-line* data (see Chap. 5). In this chapter a general overview of both off-line and on-line HTR is presented in Sec. 3.2 and Sec. 3.3, respectively. The corresponding *baseline* recognizers are assessed using the off-line and on-line corpora described in Chap. 2.

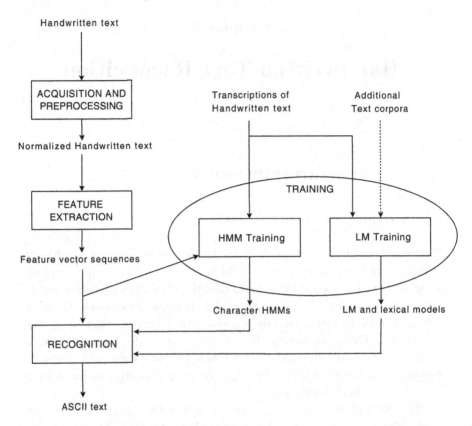

Fig. 3.1   Overview of a HTR recognizer.

Both, the off-line and the on-line HTR recognizers presented in this chapter follow a classical architecture composed of three main modules: preprocessing, feature extraction and recognition. The preprocessing module is in charge to reduce the variability of text styles. In the feature extraction module a feature vector sequence is obtained as the representation of a handwritten text image or pen trajectory. And the recognition module obtains the most likely word sequence for the sequence of feature vectors. In addition, there is another module devoted to train the different models used on the recognition step: Hidden Markov Models, n-gram language models and lexical models. Fig. 3.1 shows a diagram of this architecture. It needs to be mentioned that the recognition module discussed in this chapter will be adapted in Chap. 4 in order to cope with interactively produced validated prefixes.

3.2 Off-line Handwritten Text Recognition

This section presents the off-line HTR recognizer used in this work. The following three subsections describe each of the main modules (preprocessing, feature extraction and recognition) in detail. Then, the different experiments carried out, the assessment measures used and the results obtained are explained in Subsections 3.2.4 and 3.2.6.

3.2.1 *Preprocessing*

It is quite common that handwritten documents, and specially ancient documents, suffer from degradation problems [Drida (2006)]. In addition, other kinds of difficulties appear in these pages, such as different font types and word sizes, underlined and/or crossed-out words, etc. The combination of these problems contribute to make the recognition process difficult, therefore a preprocessing module becomes essential.

There is not a general, standard preprocessing approach, and it can be said that each handwriting recognition system has its own, particular solution. In the preprocessing module used in this work the following steps take place: background removal and noise reduction, skew correction, line extraction, slope correction, slant correction and size normalization.

Note that the IAMDB and ODEC corpora are used at sentence level, so the skew correction and line extraction operations will only be applied to the CS corpus.

Background removal and noise reduction Degradation problems that often appear in handwritten documents are factors that impede (in many cases may disable) their legibility. Therefore, appropriate filtering methods are needed to remove noise, improve quality and make the documents more legible. Within this framework, noise is considered anything that is irrelevant for the textual information (i.e, the foreground) of the document image.

In this work, background removal and noise reduction are performed by applying a 2-dimensional median filter [Kavallieratou and Stamatatos (2006)] on the entire image and subtracting the result from the original image. Then, a grey-level normalization to increase the foreground/background image contrast is applied (see Fig. 3.2).

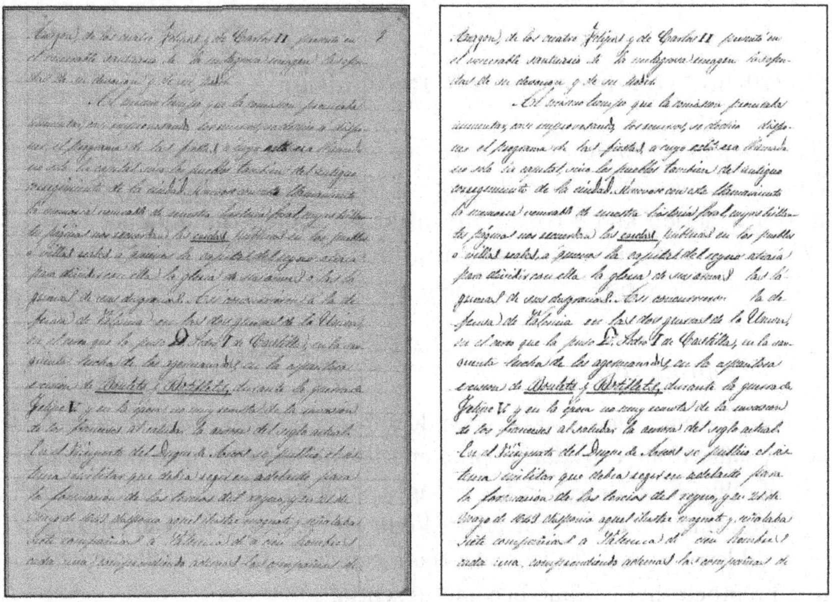

Fig. 3.2 Background removal, noise reduction, increase of contrast and skew correction example: a) original image; b) preprocessed image.

Skew correction The skew is a distortion introduced during the document scanning process. It is understood as the angle of the document paper with respect to the scanner coordinates system. So, skew correction must be carried out on each whole document image, by aligning the text lines with the horizontal direction. This process makes the line and paragraph extraction easier.

While some authors do refer to this misframing as skew [Amin and Ficher (2000); Bunke (2003); Cao *et al.* (2003)], others define skew as the angle between the horizontal direction and the direction of the line on which the writer aligns the words (this is called "slope" in this work [Vinciarelli (2002); Morita *et al.* (1999)]), and some authors use it interchangeably to refer to the misframing of the entire page, and for the wrong alignment of the words with the horizontal direction.

The skew correction is carried out by searching for the angle which maximizes the variance of the horizontal projection profile and then apply a rotation operation with this angle [Pastor (2007)]. Figure 3.2 (right) illustrates a page image after background removal, noise reduction, increase of contrast and skew correction.

Line extraction The next step consists in dividing the page image into separate line images. The method used is based on the horizontal projection profile of the input image. Local minima in this projection are considered as potential cut-points located between consecutive text lines. When the minimum values are greater than zero, no clear separation is possible. This problem is solved using a method based on connected components [Marti and Bunke (2001)].

Figure 3.3 (right) shows the resulting line images extracted from the highlighted region in the page image of the left after applying the method above mentioned. In Fig. 3.4 (top) we can see in more detail one of the resulting line images.

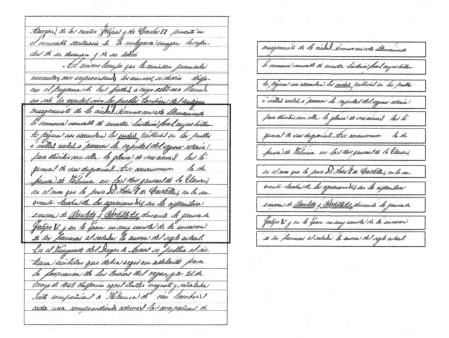

Fig. 3.3 Line extraction example: Left) Image with cutting lines; Right) separated line images from the highlighted region.

Slope correction   The slope is the angle between the horizontal direction and the direction of the line on which the writer aligned each word or text segment on a line. Since each word or multiword segment in the text line may have a different slope angle, the original image is divided into segments surrounded by wide blank spaces and slope correction is applied to each segment separately. This is not intended to obtain a segmentation of the text line into words and it is not necessary for each segment to contain exactly one word.

This division is usually based on more or less sophisticated heuristics. A minimum size of blank space is used to define text segments. In this work, to define this minimum blank space, a vertical projection of the image is carried out and the average size of all the spaces is computed. All space of the projection for which the gray level is below a threshold will be considered blank space.

To obtain the slope angle of each segment we use a method based on horizontal projections, very similar to the method used on the skew correction operation [Pastor (2007); Toselli *et al.* (2004a)]. Once the slope of a segment has been determined, the segment is rotated with this angle but in the opposite direction.

Slant correction   Slant correction shears each isolated line segment horizontally to bring the writing in an upright position. The slant angle is determined using a method based on vertical projection profile (see [Pastor *et al.* (2004, 2006)]). The method is based on the observation that the columns distribution of the vertical projection profile present a maximum variance for the non slanted text. Figure 3.4 (middle) shows an example of an image after applying the slant correction operation.

Size normalization   The purpose of this preprocessing operation is to make the system as much invariant as possible to character size and to reduce the areas of background pixels which remain on the image because of the ascenders and descenders of some letters. Since each word (or group of words) can have a different height, the original image is divided into segments surrounded by wide blank spaces in the same way as it is explained for the slope correction. Then, upper and lower lines of each segment are computed. For this purpose, the "Run-Length Smoothing algorithm" (RLSA) [Wong *et al.* (1982)] is applied and upper and lower contours are detected for each segment. Then, the eigenvector line fitting algorithm [Duda and Hart (1973)] is applied to the contour points to compute upper and lower baselines. These lines separate the whole main text body from the zones including ascenders and descenders.

In order to obtain an uniform text line, i.e. where all their segments have the same height, it is necessary to set the same normalization height for all the main body segments. To this end, we compute the average size of the main body of all the segments and linearly scale the main body heights of each segment to this value. Finally, the ascenders and descenders are linearly scaled in height to a size determined as an empirically chosen percentage of the new main body vertical size (30% for ascenders and 15% for descenders). Since these zones are often huge blank areas, this scaling operation has the effect of filtering out most of the uninformative image background. It also reduces the large height variability of the ascenders and descenders as compared with that of the main text body [Romero *et al.* (2006)].

The image on the bottom of the Fig. 3.4 shows this last step in the preprocessing module.

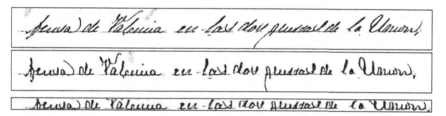

Fig. 3.4   Slant and size normalization example: Top) A separated line image; Middle) Slant correction; Bottom) Size normalization.

3.2.2   *Feature Extraction*

Our HTR recognizer is based on HMMs (see Chap. 1), therefore, each preprocessed text line image has to be represented as a sequence of feature vectors. Several approaches have been proposed to obtain this kind of sequences [Bazzi *et al.* (1999); Marti and Bunke (2001); Brakensiek *et al.* (2000)]. The approach used in this book follows the ideas initially described in [Bazzi *et al.* (1999)].

First, given a text line image of $n_r \times n_c$ pixels, a grid is applied to divide the text line image into $N \times M$ rectangular cells. N is chosen empirically, whereas M is computed as $M = \rho \frac{n_c N}{n_r}$, where ρ is tuned empirically. Each cell of the grid is characterized by the following features:

(1) Normalized gray level
(2) Horizontal component of the gray level gradient
(3) Vertical component of the gray level gradient

The normalized gray level provides information about the trace density on the analysed cell. On the other hand, the gradient gives information about how this density varies along different directions.

To obtain smoothed values of these features, feature extraction is not restricted to the cell under analysis, but extended to a $r \times s$ cells window, centred at the current cell. The values of r and s are chosen empirically.

To compute the normalized gray level, the analysis window is smoothed by convolution with two 1-d Gaussian filters. Thus, the gray level of each pixel affected by the Gaussian, on an analysis window with $n \times m$ pixels, where $n = \frac{n_r}{N}r$ and $m = \frac{n_c}{M}s$ is computed as:

$$I'(i,j) = I(i,j) \; \exp\left[-\frac{1}{2}\left(\frac{(i-n/2)^2}{(n/4)^2} + \frac{(j-m/2)^2}{(m/4)^2} \right) \right]$$

Finally, the gray level for the cell under analysis is computed as the average of the gray level from the pixels in the window:

$$g = \frac{\sum_{i=0}^{n-1}\sum_{j=0}^{m-1} I'(i,j)}{nm}$$

The horizontal component of the gray level gradient, d_h, is calculated as the slope of the line which best fits the horizontal function of column-average gray level in the analysis window. The fitting criterion is the sum of squared errors weighted by a 1-d Gaussian filter which enhances the role of central pixels of the window under analysis:

$$d_h = \frac{(\sum_{j=0}^{m-1} w_j g_j)(\sum_{j=0}^{m-1} w_j j) - (\sum_{j=0}^{m-1} w_j)(\sum_{j=0}^{m-1} w_j g_j j)}{(\sum_{j=0}^{m-1} w_j j)^2 - (\sum_{j=0}^{m-1} w_j)(\sum_{j=0}^{m-1} w_j j^2)}$$

where g_j is, in this case, the column-average gray level at column j, defined as:

$$g_j = \frac{\sum_{i=0}^{n-1} I(i,j)}{n}$$

The vertical gradient component, d_v, is computed in a similar way.

Columns of cells (also called *frames*) are processed from left to right and a feature vector is constructed for each *frame* by stacking the three features computed in their constituent cells. Hence, at the end of this process, a sequence of M {$3N$}-dimensional feature vectors (N normalized gray-level components and N horizontal and vertical gradient components) is obtained. In Fig. 3.5 an example of the feature vectors sequence for a fraction of a separate line image is shown graphically.

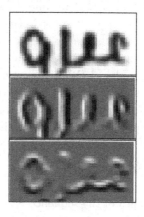

Fig. 3.5 Example of the feature vectors sequence for a portion of a line image.

3.2.3 *Recognition*

Probabilistic Framework As explained before, a handwritten sentence image can be represented as a sequence of any number M of feature vectors, each of dimension $3N$, $\mathbf{x} = \vec{x}_1 \, \vec{x}_2 \, \ldots \, \vec{x}_M$, $\vec{x}_i \in \Re^{3N}$. Therefore, traditional handwritten text recognition can be formulated as the problem of finding a most likely word sequence, $\mathbf{w} = w_1 \, w_2 \, \ldots \, w_l$, for the given input image $\mathbf{x}$:

$$\hat{\mathbf{w}} = \operatorname*{argmax}_{\mathbf{w}} \Pr(\mathbf{w} \mid \mathbf{x}) \tag{3.1}$$

Using the Bayes' rule:

$$\hat{\mathbf{w}} = \operatorname*{argmax}_{\mathbf{w}} \frac{\Pr(\mathbf{x} \mid \mathbf{w}) \Pr(\mathbf{w})}{\Pr(\mathbf{x})} \tag{3.2}$$

Since, $\Pr(\mathbf{x})$ does not depend on the maximisation variable, $\mathbf{w}$, it can be dropped. Thus, the probability $\Pr(\mathbf{w} \mid \mathbf{x})$ is decomposed into two probabilities, $\Pr(\mathbf{x} \mid \mathbf{w})$ and $\Pr(\mathbf{w})$, representing morphological-lexical knowledge and syntactic knowledge, respectively:

$$\hat{\mathbf{w}} = \operatorname*{argmax}_{\mathbf{w}} \Pr(\mathbf{x} \mid \mathbf{w}) \Pr(\mathbf{w}) \approx \operatorname*{argmax}_{\mathbf{w}} P(\mathbf{x} \mid \mathbf{w}) P(\mathbf{w}) \tag{3.3}$$

$\Pr(\mathbf{x} \mid \mathbf{w})$ is approximated as $P(\mathbf{x} \mid \mathbf{w})$, typically by concatenating character models, usually Hidden Markov Models [Jelinek (1998); Rabiner (1989)]. On the other hand, $\Pr(\mathbf{w})$ is approximated by a word language model, $P(\mathbf{w})$, usually n-grams [Jelinek (1998)].

In practice, the product of $P(\mathbf{x} \mid \mathbf{w})$ and $P(\mathbf{w})$ needs to be modified in order to balance the absolute values of both probabilities. The most common modification is to use a language weight α (Grammar Scale Factor, GSF), which weights the influence of the language model in the recognition result, and an insertion penalty β (Word Insertion Penalty, WIP), which helps to control the word insertion rate of the recognizer [Ogawa *et al.* (1998)]. In addition, we use log-probabilities to avoid the numeric underflow problems that can appear using probabilities. So, Eq. (3.3) can be rewritten as:

$$\hat{\mathbf{w}} = \operatorname*{argmax}_{\mathbf{w}} \; log \, P(\mathbf{x} \mid \mathbf{w}) + \alpha \; log \, P(\mathbf{w}) + l(\mathbf{w})\beta \qquad (3.4)$$

where $l(\mathbf{w})$ is the word length of the sequence $\mathbf{w}$ and the parameters α and β are tuned empirically.

Character, Word and Language Modelling   HMMs have received significant attention in handwriting recognition during the last few years. As in speech recognizers for acoustic data [Rabiner and Juang (1993)], HMMs are used to estimate the probability of a sequence of feature vectors representing a handwritten text image. Sentence models are built by concatenation of word models which, in turn, are often obtained by concatenation of continuous HMMs for individual characters.

Basically, each character HMM is a stochastic finite-state device that models the succession, along the horizontal axis, of feature vectors which are extracted from images of this character (see Sec. 1.3.1 for a formal definition of HMM). Each HMM state generates feature vectors following an adequate parametric probabilistic law; typically, a Gaussian Mixture.

The required number of Gaussians in the mixture depends, among many other factors, on the vertical variability typically associated with each state. On the other hand, the adequate number of states to model a certain character depends on the underlying horizontal variability. For instance, to ideally model a capital "H" character, only three states might be enough (one to model the first vertical bar, other for the horizontal line, and finally the other for the last vertical bar). Note that the possible or optional blank space that may appear between characters should be also modelled by each character HMM. The number of states and Gaussians define the total amount of parameters to be estimated. Therefore, these numbers need to be empirically tuned to optimize the overall performance for the given amount of training vectors available.

Taking this into account, the HMMs have two implicit stochastical process: one of them describes the different parts that conform the object (character) and the other the variability of these parts. Left-to-right HMMs are adequate for HTR, given the horizontal direction of the process of extraction of feature vectors. In these models a transition between two HMM states, $q_i, q_j \in Q$, is only possible if $j \geq i$. Figure 3.6 shows an example of how a HMM models two feature vector subsequences corresponding to the character "a".

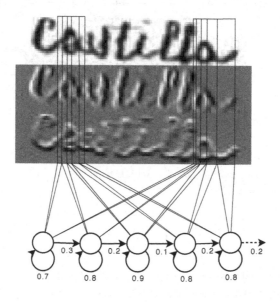

Fig. 3.6   Example of a 5-states HMM modelling (feature vectors sequences of) instances of the character "a" within the Spanish word "Castilla". The states are shared among all instances of characters of the same class.

Once a HMM topology (number of states and structure) has been adopted, the model parameters can be easily trained from images of continuously handwritten text (without any kind of segmentation) accompanied by the transcription of these images into the corresponding sequence of characters. This training process is carried out using a well known instance of the EM algorithm called forward backward or Baum-Welch (see Sec. 1.3.1).

The concatenation of characters to form words is modelled by simple lexical models. Each word is modelled by a stochastic finite-state automaton which represents all possible concatenations of individual characters that may compose the word. This automaton takes into account optional character capitalizations. By embedding the character HMMs into the edges of this automaton, a *lexical HMM* is obtained. These HMMs estimate the word-conditional probability $\Pr(\mathbf{x}|\mathbf{w})$ of Eq. 3.3. An example of automaton for the word "the" is shown in Fig. 3.7:

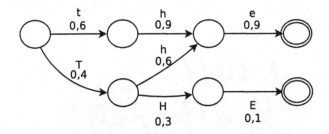

Fig. 3.7   Automaton for the lexicon entry "the".

Finally, the concatenation of words into text lines or sentences is modelled by an n-gram *language model*, which uses the previous $n-1$ words to predict the next one; that is,

$$\Pr(\mathbf{w}) \approx \prod_{i=1}^{N} P(w_i \mid \mathbf{w}_{i-n+1}^{i-1}) \tag{3.5}$$

N-gram models, with Kneser-Ney back-off smoothing [Katz (1987); Kneser and Ney (1995)], estimate the probability $\Pr(\mathbf{w})$ in Eq. (3.3) (see Sec. 1.3.2). A simple example of LM is shown in Fig. 3.8:

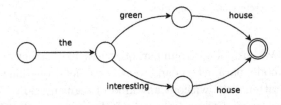

Fig. 3.8   A simple language model.

Once all the *character, word* and *language* models are available, recognition of new test sentences can be performed. Thanks to the homogeneous finite-state (FS) nature of all these models, they can be easily *integrated* into a single *global* FS model by replacing each word of the n-gram model with its corresponding lexical model and the edges of the lexical model with the corresponding character HMMs. The search for decoding the input feature vectors sequence $\mathbf{x}$ into the output words sequence $\hat{\mathbf{w}}$, is performed over this global model by using the Viterbi algorithm [Jelinek (1998)]. This algorithm can be easily adapted also for the search required in the interactive framework explained in Chap. 4.

All the above recognition process has been described at word level; that is, the recognition result is expressed as a sequence of words. However, it can be similarly done at character level by replacing $\mathbf{w}$ whit $\mathbf{c}$ in the Eq. 3.3, where $\mathbf{c}$ is now a sequence of characters. Therefore, now the problem can be formulated as the problem of finding the most likely character sequence $\mathbf{c}$, for the given feature vector sequence $\mathbf{x}$:

$$\hat{\mathbf{c}} = \underset{\mathbf{c}}{\operatorname{argmax}} \Pr(\mathbf{x} \mid \mathbf{c}) \Pr(\mathbf{c}) \approx \underset{\mathbf{c}}{\operatorname{argmax}} P(\mathbf{x} \mid \mathbf{c}) P(\mathbf{c}) \qquad (3.6)$$

$\Pr(\mathbf{x} \mid \mathbf{c})$ can be directly modelled by Hidden Markov Models and $\Pr(\mathbf{c})$ is approximated by character n-grams.

In this case, the n-grams model the way in which the characters can be concatenated into text lines or sentences. It is important to note that now there are no lexicon models: both lexical and syntactic constraints are jointly modelled by the n-grams. In order to capture lexical constraints, the n-gram order has to be high enough (larger than the average word length).

Character level HTR is a relatively new and promising idea when the task lexicon is not fully available and "open vocabulary" must be assumed. Character n-grams do not have lexicon-related limitations and any character sequence appearing in the handwritten text images can be recognized. However, if all (or most of) the relevant word forms are known, it is very clear that dictionary-based, explicit lexicon models impose lexical constraints much more accurately than character n-grams trained from a text corpus.

On the other hand, in the interactive transcription process presented in the next chapter we study interactions at the character level, which might become much simpler if the underlying HTR recognizer could also work directly at the character level.

It is for these reasons that, in this chapter, we want to assess the capabilities of an HTR recognizer using character n-grams.

3.2.4   *Experimental Framework*

The experimental framework adopted to assess the effectiveness of the off-line HTR recognizer is described in the following subsections. They include details of the different corpora, the performance measures used and a discussion about the values used for the different meta-parameters tested on the experiments.

Corpora   Experiments have been carried out using the three different off-line corpora explained in the Chap. 2.

To train the character HMMs of the different corpora, we consider all the elements appearing in each handwritten text image of the training set, such as lowercase and uppercase letters, symbols, abbreviations, spacing between words and characters, crossed-words, etc. However, to train the n-gram models we imposed certain usual/useful restrictions intended to simplify the experiments and additionally allowing them to be fully reproducible. This restriction consist in converting uppercase character to lowercase and eliminating the punctuation signs. In the CS and ODEC corpora, only the text corresponding to the training partition has been used to train the n-grams. The words of the test partition that do not appear in the training text are added to the training vocabulary and considered as singletons. In this way, we are working with closed vocabulary. The number of words of the test partition that do not appear on the train partition is shown in the column OOV of the tables that summarize the corpora features in the Chap. 2.

For the IAM dataset the training of the n-grams is not restricted only to the text transcription of the train sentences, but the full LOB, Brown and Wellington text corpora have been used after removing the test sentences.

Assessment Measures   Two different measures have been used to asses the quality of the transcriptions obtained. These measures are the well known word error rate (WER) and the character error rate (CER).

The WER is based on counting the number of word differences between the transcriptions proposed by the system and the reference transcriptions. This measure has been used to assess the accuracy of automatic speech recognition (ASR) systems. The computation of this measure is not trivial, because the hypotheses length can be different from the reference length.

Therefore, the WER is defined by means of an alignment between the two word sequences. In this alignment 4 different situations can occur:

- **correct word:** the reference word coincides with the aligned hypothesis word.
- **substitution:** the reference word is aligned with a different word from the hypothesis.
- **insertion:** a word has been inserted in the hypothesis that can not be aligned with any word from the reference.
- **deletion:** a reference word does not appear in the hypothesis.

The optimal alignment is defined as the alignment that minimizes the *Levenshtein* distance [Sankoff and Kruskal (1983)]; i.e., the minimum number of insertions, deletions and substitutions between the two word sequences. This value can be obtained using dynamic programming. Therefore, the WER is defined as the minimum number of words that need to be substituted, deleted or inserted to convert a sentence recognized by the system into the corresponding reference transcription, divided by the total number of words in the reference transcription:

$$\text{WER} = 100 \cdot \frac{N_i + N_s + N_d}{N_s + N_d + N_c}$$

where N_i is the number of insertions; N_s is the number of substitutions; N_d is the number of deletions and N_c is the number of correct words.

Note, that if the number of insertion is very high, the WER can be greater than 100%.

The definition of the CER is analogous to the WER, but replacing words with characters.

Meta-parameters There are some basic meta-parameters that need to be adjusted to design an accurate recognizer with our approach. They are:

- N: is the vertical number of cells in which the image is divided.
- ρ: is the factor used to determine the number of horizontal cells in which each image is divided.
- $r \times s$: is the size of the analysis window used during the feature extraction process.
- N_S: is the number of states for each character HMM.
- N_G: is the number of Gaussian densities used in each state of the HMM.

- α: is the grammar scale factor.
- β: is the word insertion penalty.

Automatic determination of optimal values for these meta-parameters is not easy. In particular, it is difficult to determine independent, optimal values of N_S and N_G for each character HMM. For simplicity, we decided to use the same values of N_S and N_G for all HMMs. The best meta-parameter values were empirically tuned for each task.

Feature extraction was applied to the preprocessed databases to obtain a sequence of $(3N)$-dimensional feature vectors for each handwritten image. As discussed in Sec. 3.2.3, left to right continuous density HMMs of N_S states and N_G Gaussian densities per state were used for character modelling. Each HMM has only two transitions per state (one to the same state and the other one to the next state). In addition, a diagonal covariance matrix for each Gaussian in the mixture was used. These HMMs were trained through four iterations of the Baum-Welch algorithm. For each test sentence, the Viterbi algorithm was performed on the integrated finite-state network to obtain the desired recognized transcription.

Another meta-parameter that must be adjusted is the order of the n-gram language model. Here, we have carried out experiments using language models at word level and at character level. Taking into account previous results we decided to test the word language model using bi-grams. However, to test the language model at character level orders ranging from 2 to 9 were considered.

3.2.5   *Meta-parameter Adjustment Experiments*

Different experiments, with the three off-line corpora described in Chapter 2, have been carried out to fix adequate values of the studied meta-parameters, in order to obtain good results for each task and to study the sensitivity of the recognizer accuracy by varying the values of these meta-parameters. In this subsection the results obtained for the different task using n-grams at word level are detailed.

CS corpus   To obtain the best result with the CS corpus we have tested different values for the meta-parameters that need to be optimized. First, we have optimized the values of the meta-parameters N, ρ, $r \times s$ and N_S. Once this values have been fixed, the meta-parameters N_G, α and β for the page and the book partition have been optimized independently.

The tested values for the meta-parameters N, ρ, $r \times s$ and N_S are:

- $N = 16$, 20 and 24.
- $\rho = 1$, 2 and 3.
- $r \times s = 5 \times 5$, 5×9, 9×5, 9×9, 9×11, 11×9 and 11×11.
- $N_S = 6$, 8, 10, 12 and 14

As previously explained, automatic determination of optimal values for these meta-parameters is not an easy task. In particular, it is difficult to determine independent, optimal values of N_S and N_G for each character HMM. For simplicity, we decided to use the same values of N_S and N_G for all HMMs.

Table 3.1 shows the HTR WER(%) obtained for the CS corpus in its page partition for $N = 16$ and different values of the meta-parameters ρ, $r \times s$ and N_S. Similar experiments are shown in Tables 3.2 and 3.3 for $N = 20$ and $N = 24$ respectively.

Table 3.1   Performance of the basic off-line HTR recognizer for $N = 16$ and different values of the meta-parameters ρ, $r \times s$ and N_S in the CS corpus in its page partition.

N	ρ	N_S	$r \times s$						
			5×5	5×9	9×5	9×9	9×11	11×9	11×11
16	1	6	69.1	67.3	67.4	63.7	66.4	64.0	66.5
		8	83.6	79.3	80.1	78.9	78.8	78.9	79.6
		10	97.7	96.3	98.1	96.7	96.7	96.9	97.0
		12	98.6	98.1	98.6	98.1	98.1	98.6	98.2
		14	96.9	95.8	97.5	96.5	96.5	97.0	98.1
	2	6	43.5	38.5	39.2	38.5	38.2	39.9	40.9
		8	39.9	37.7	37.5	36.2	37.2	37.6	38.1
		10	39.2	36.3	35.9	36.7	37.6	38.2	38.7
		12	41.0	40.1	38.4	38.2	37.6	39.9	41.0
		14	48.0	45.5	46.1	45.1	39.7	46.1	46.0
	3	6	39.6	37.8	36.7	35.6	35.3	36.2	36.9
		8	37.2	33.6	34.3	33.1	33.4	33.8	34.6
		10	34.3	32.7	31.3	31.6	32.1	32.9	33.8
		12	31.8	31.5	30.7	30.7	30.8	31.3	32.1
		14	32.5	32.1	31.6	31.4	32.2	31.7	32.7

The best WER, 30.5%, has been obtained using $N = 20$ and $\rho = 3$. The size of the analysis window is 9×5 and the number of states is 12. Now, we are going to use this baseline to continue looking for the best value of the meta-parameters N_G, α and β.

In Table 3.4 we can see the results for the meta-parameters values: $N_G = 32, 64, 128$; $\alpha = 60, 70, 80, 90, 100$ and $\beta = -120, -140, -160, -180$.

Table 3.2 Performance of the basic off-line HTR recognizer for $N = 20$ and different values of the meta-parameters ρ, $r \times s$ and N_S in the CS corpus in its page partition.

N	ρ	N_S	$r \times s$						
			5×5	5×9	9×5	9×9	9×11	11×9	11×11
20	1	6	50.4	48.0	44.5	44.1	45.6	44.7	46.4
		8	52.6	49.0	47.4	47.2	49.1	48.1	49.7
		10	69.2	64.6	65.9	64.0	63.6	36.9	64.8
		12	93.1	90.5	91.7	89.6	88.8	90.9	89.6
		14	98.8	97.5	98.6	97.7	97.3	97.5	96.4
	2	6	40.9	37.6	35.4	33.9	34.3	35.6	35.8
		8	35.1	35.5	32.6	37.6	32.9	33.4	33.1
		10	34.9	33.7	31.8	31.3	31.8	32.0	33.2
		12	34.3	33.3	30.9	31.7	32.2	31.7	33.1
		14	35.4	34.6	32.1	33.1	33.5	33.0	34.2
	3	6	41.4	40.7	39.3	37.7	37.8	40.3	39.9
		8	37.0	36.2	34.6	34.0	34.5	35.7	36.1
		10	35.5	34.5	32.3	32.6	32.9	33.3	34.0
		12	34.0	33.2	**30.5**	30.9	31.5	30.4	32.6
		14	34.9	34.5	32.0	32.1	32.0	32.8	33.4

The best result, 28.5%, is obtained for $N_G = 32$, $\alpha = 90$ and $\beta = -140$.

For the CS corpus in its book partition we assume that the best values of the meta-parameters for the feature extraction module are the same previously tuned on the CS corpus for its page partition. However, the bi-gram language model trained in this case will be different to the bi-gram trained on the page partition. So, we need to tune the meta-parameters α and β for this partition. In Table 3.5 we can see the results obtained for different values of the meta-parameters: $N_G = 32$, 64 and 128, $\alpha = 60$, 70, 80 and 90 and $\beta = -140, -160, -180$. The best results, 33.5% is obtained for the values $N_G = 32$, $GSF = 80$ and $WIP = -160$.

ODEC corpus Similar experiments have been carried out with the ODEC corpora. The tested values for the meta-parameters N, ρ, $r \times s$ and N_S are:

- $N = 16$, 20 and 24.
- $\rho = 1$ and 2.
- $r \times s = 3 \times 3$, 3×5, 5×3, 5×5, 5×9, 9×5 and 9×9.
- $N_S = 4$, 6 and 8.

Table 3.3 Performance of the basic off-line HTR recognizer for $N = 24$ and different values of the meta-parameters ρ, $r \times s$ and N_S in the CS corpus in its page partition.

N	ρ	N_S	$r \times s$						
			5×5	5×9	9×5	9×9	9×11	11×9	11×11
		6	44.4	39.7	36.7	35.9	37.9	36.0	38.0
		8	42.4	40.2	36.6	36.7	37.9	37.2	37.9
	1	10	45.8	44.3	41.1	41.5	42.8	41.4	43.5
		12	62.1	59.1	58.0	55.8	57.1	56.2	57.9
		14	85.8	82.0	84.2	80.8	79.7	80.5	79.9
		6	41.3	38.9	37.2	36.5	35.6	36.2	36.8
		8	38.8	36.2	34.0	34.5	33.8	32.2	33.4
24	2	10	34.4	33.7	31.1	31.2	31.6	31.7	32.1
		12	34.6	33.9	31.2	31.7	31.6	31.5	32.0
		14	34.7	34.4	32.4	32.8	31.0	31.6	31.3
		6	46.6	44.5	46.6	46.3	46.0	47.1	47.3
		8	41.9	41.1	39.6	38.6	40.4	41.5	41.4
	3	10	38.6	37.9	36.3	36.3	37.5	37.2	38.2
		12	37.1	36.2	33.4	34.4	35.7	34.5	35.2
		14	36.2	35.0	32.8	33.2	33.2	32.9	33.1

Table 3.6 show the HTR WER(%) obtained for the ODEC corpora for the different values of the meta-parameters previously defined. The values of the meta-parameters that obtain the best result on this table are fixed in the experiments to look for the best N_G, α and β. In Table 3.7 we can see the results obtained with different values of these meta-parameters, $N_G = 32$, 64 and 128; $\alpha = 10$, 20, 40 and 60; and $\beta = 0$, -10 and -20. The best result (22.9%) has been obtained using $N = 16$, $\rho = 1$, $r \times s = 5 \times 3$, $N_S = 6$, $N_G = 32$, $\alpha = 20$ and $\beta = -10$.

IAMDB corpus As in the other two corpora first we have optimized the value of the meta-parameters N, ρ, $r \times s$ and N_S, and once this values are fixed, we continue looking for the best value of the meta-parameters N_G, α and β. Table 3.8 shows the HTR WER(%) obtained for the IAMDB corpora for $N = 16$, 20 and 24; $\rho = 1$ and 2; $r \times s = 3 \times 3$, 3×5, 5×3, 5×5, 5×9, 9×5 and 9×9 and $N_S = 4$, 6 and 8.

In Table 3.9 we can see the results obtained for different values of the meta-parameters N_G, α and β. The best result (25.3%) is obtained using $N = 20$, $\rho = 1$, $r \times s = 5 \times 5$, $N_S = 6$, $N_G = 64$, $\alpha = 40$ and $\beta = 0$.

Table 3.4 Performance of the basic off-line HTR system for different values of the meta-parameters α, N_G and β on the CS corpora on its page partition.

N_G	β	α				
		60	70	80	90	100
32	-120	30.6	29.8	29.3	28.6	28.7
	-140	30.2	29.5	29.1	**28.5**	28.6
	-160	30.0	29.6	29.1	28.6	28.6
	-180	29.9	29.4	29.8	28.6	28.7
64	-120	31.7	31.1	30.7	30.5	30.4
	-140	31.6	31.0	30.7	30.3	30.3
	-160	31.6	30.9	30.5	30.3	30.3
	-180	31.4	30.8	30.7	30.4	30.3
128	-120	36.7	35.5	35.4	35.3	35.3
	-140	36.2	35.4	36.7	35.2	35.3
	-160	35.8	35.4	34.2	35.0	35.1
	-180	35.5	35.1	35.2	35.3	35.2

Table 3.5 Performance of the basic off-line HTR system for different values of the meta-parameters α, N_G and β on the CS corpora on its book partition.

N_G	β	α			
		60	70	80	90
32	-140	34.6	34.0	33.7	33.7
	-160	34.5	33.9	**33.5**	33.6
	-180	34.3	33.7	33.6	33.8
64	-140	37.3	36.9	36.0	35.9
	-160	37.2	36.5	36.1	35.9
	-180	37.0	36.6	36.1	36.0
128	-140	41.3	41.1	40.6	40.3
	-160	40.9	41.0	40.3	40.1
	-180	40.9	40.8	40.1	40.0

3.2.6 *Discussion of Results*

In this subsection we summarize and discuss the results presented in the previous subsection.

Results with word language models Figure 3.9 shows the HTR WER(%) obtained for the page partition of the corpus CS, as a function of the number of states per HMM ($N_S = 6, 8, 10, 12, 14$), for different values

Table 3.6 Performance of the basic off-line HTR system different values of the meta-parameters N, ρ, $r \times s$ and N_S on the ODEC corpora.

N	ρ	N_S	$r \times s$						
			3×3	3×5	5×3	5×5	5×9	9×5	9×9
16	1	4	29.6	30.7	27.5	30.8	42.9	36.0	56.2
		6	24.7	26.4	**23.2**	26.8	39.3	30.6	49.6
		8	41.5	41.9	41.4	42.0	48.5	46.2	57.6
	2	4	54.1	50.7	51.3	48.8	50.0	49.3	59.0
		6	32.3	32.7	35.9	34.2	43.2	36.9	42.4
		8	26.8	26.5	25.5	24.5	33.1	25.0	34.1
20	1	4	36.2	35.5	33.7	35.9	88.8	37.3	52.3
		6	27.0	27.3	24.1	26.0	45.3	27.3	41.4
		8	28.1	28.0	26.6	27.5	34.4	29.1	39.7
	2	4	75.3	73.1	68.9	43.5	62.0	70.0	63.7
		6	75.7	78.5	65.2	57.4	42.1	55.3	45.1
		8	80.1	76.3	56.7	42.3	34.0	49.7	36.3
24	1	4	48.3	45.1	45.6	42.3	48.5	50.1	54.1
		6	32.8	32.0	29.3	30.0	35.9	31.6	38.4
		8	26.6	27.2	25.3	26.0	31.6	26.8	32.9
	2	4	97.0	98.3	98.0	97.0	88.5	83.0	88.5
		6	73.4	70.2	64.8	63.0	53.5	60.3	60.0
		8	98.6	98.0	98.2	89.2	89.0	85.4	56.0

of the vertical dimension $N = 16, 20, 24$, and aspect ratio factor $\rho = 2$ (left) and $\rho = 3$ (right). The size of the analysis window used here is 9×5, that is the size that has provided the best results.

The best WER, 30.5%, was obtained using $N = 20$, $N_S = 12$ and $\rho = 3$. From now on, this baseline will be used to continue looking for the best value of the other meta-parameters N_G, α and β. As previously said, the tested values of these meta-parameters are: $N_G = 32, 64, 128$; $\alpha = 60, 70, 80, 90, 100$ and $\beta = -140, -160, -180$. Fig. 3.10 shows the evolution of WER for an increasing value of the grammar scale factor α and different values of the word insertion penalty β, setting the number of Gaussian mixture components N_G to 32. The best result, 28.5% was obtained for $\alpha = 90$ and $\beta = -140$. This result will be the baseline for the experiments carried out on the next chapters.

For the book partition of CS corpus we assume that the best values of the feature extraction meta-parameters are the same previously tuned on the CS page partition. The bi-gram language model trained in this case is different from the bi-gram trained for the page partition. So, we need

Table 3.7 Performance of the basic off-line HTR system for different values of the meta-parameters α, N_G and β on the ODEC corpora.

N_G	β	α			
		10	20	40	60
	0	26.6	23.1	26.7	34.7
32	-10	25.8	**22.9**	27.4	35.0
	-20	25.7	23.0	27.6	35.8
	0	26.3	23.2	26.9	34.5
64	-10	26.1	23.1	27.1	34.9
	-20	25.9	23.4	27.5	35.9
	0	29.6	26.3	28.7	36.4
128	-10	29.2	26.2	29.3	36.9
	-20	28.8	26.3	29.8	37.4

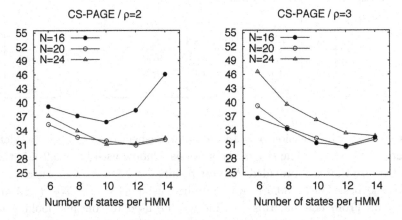

Fig. 3.9 WER (%) for varying number of states per HMM and different values of the vertical dimension N. The aspect ratio factor was $\rho = 2$ for the left graph, and $\rho = 3$ for the right one. In both cases, the analysis window size was $r \times s = 9 \times 5$.

to tune the meta-parameters α and β for this partition. Fig. 3.11 shows the WER obtained as a function of the grammar scale factor α for different values of the word insertion penalty β. The best result, 33.5% was obtained for $\alpha = 80$ and $\beta = -160$. These values will be used as baseline for the experiments carried out on the next chapters.

As expected, the results obtained with the CS page partition were better than those of the book partition. This is mainly due to the fact that the test text line samples of the page partition were extracted from the same

Table 3.8 Performance of the basic off-line HTR system different values of the meta-parameters N, ρ, $r \times s$ and N_S on the IAMDB corpora.

N	ρ	N_S	$r \times s$						
			3×3	3×5	5×3	5×5	5×9	9×5	9×9
16	1	4	36.5	36.0	36.6	35.3	40.4	40.4	49.4
		6	31.4	29.8	29.8	29.4	36.1	34.3	41.8
		8	43.0	41.8	41.3	41.0	42.8	43.2	48.6
	2	4	44.8	64.6	69.4	44.1	50.3	52.6	61.3
		6	30.9	29.8	30.0	29.8	30.8	33.4	53.8
		8	26.0	26.5	26.3	26.0	27.4	27.6	41.2
20	1	4	35.2	34.7	34.4	34.2	37.8	39.7	46.6
		6	27.5	25.8	25.5	**25.3**	29.0	27.1	34.9
		8	27.4	27.1	27.3	25.9	29.4	28.2	33.0
	2	4	68.2	60.5	64.9	62.3	58.8	58.6	73.2
		6	43.2	41.9	40.9	39.2	38.1	43.2	46.1
		8	37.5	37.3	34.1	33.4	34.0	35.2	38.8
24	1	4	41.1	40.0	39.8	40.6	41.3	41.9	47.8
		6	29.8	27.9	27.2	26.5	28.2	27.8	35.7
		8	29.3	27.6	26.9	25.8	27.6	26.4	34.7
	2	4	88.4	81.7	85.0	80.7	81.3	82.6	85.1
		6	73.2	65.7	65.1	63.7	65.2	64.7	68.6
		8	73.6	69.5	63.1	62.3	64.7	62.4	70.3

pages that the training text line samples. However, book partition better approaches a realistic transcription process as it was explained in Sec. 2.2.

Similar experiments have been carried out with the other two corpora, for the same feature extraction meta-parameters for both ODEC and IAMDB corpora. The tested values for the vertical dimension and aspect ratio factor where N were 16, 20 and 24, and $\rho = 1$ and 2, respectively. The different tested values for the analysis window size were: 3×3, 3×5, 5×3, 5×5, 5×9, 9×5 and 9×9. Finally the number of states were: $N_S = 4, 6, 8$. Tables 3.10 and 3.11 show the HTR WER(%) obtained for the ODEC and IAMDB corpora, respectively, for the different values of N_S and N, being $\rho = 1$, $r \times s = 5 \times 3$ for the ODEC corpus and 5×5 for IAMDB.

The values of the meta-parameters that obtain the best result in Tables 3.10 and 3.11 were selected for the experiments to look for the best N_G, α and β. Figs. 3.12 and 3.13 show the WER obtained for ODEC and IAMDB as a function of the Grammar Scale Factor, α, for different values of the Word Insertion Penalty, β. The values of the meta-parameters used in the ODEC corpus to obtain the best result (22.9%) are: $N = 16$, $\rho = 1$,

Table 3.9   Performance of the basic off-line HTR system for different values of the meta-parameters α, N_G and β on the IAMDB corpora.

NG	WIP	GSF			
		20	40	60	80
	10	32.9	28.1	34.0	39.2
32	0	32.3	27.9	31.2	35.3
	-10	31.4	28.3	28.0	37.2
	10	30.9	26.0	27.8	33.9
64	0	28.8	**25.3**	28.3	33.6
	-10	29.1	25.6	28.1	34.2
	10	29.0	31.1	27.9	33.1
128	0	27.5	25.4	27.7	33.5
	-10	28.1	27.6	27.9	33.6

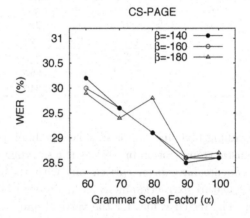

Fig. 3.10   WER for different values of the grammar scale factor α and word insertion penalty β obtained with the page partition of the CS corpus.

$r \times s = 5 \times 3$, $N_S = 6$, $N_G = 32$, $\alpha = 20$ and $\beta = -10$. For the IAMDB, the best result (25.3%) is obtained using $N = 20$, $\rho = 1$, $r \times s = 5 \times 5$, $N_S = 6$, $N_G = 64$, $\alpha = 40$ and $\beta = 0$.

Note that the best WER obtained for IAMDB (25.3%) is comparable with state-of-the art results published for this data-set. Specifically in [Zimmermann *et al.* (2006)], where similar results are reported using a system based also on HMMs and n-grams, but with a completely different feature extraction approach.

Table 3.12 summarized the best results obtained with the different cor-

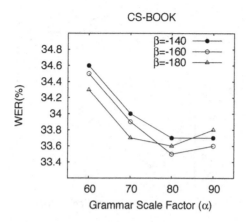

Fig. 3.11 WER for different values of the grammar scale factor α and word insertion penalty β obtained with the book partition of the CS corpora.

Table 3.10 ODEC WER of the basic off-line HTR system for different values of the number of HMM states N_S and the vertical dimension N, fixing the aspect ratio factor $\rho = 1$ and the analysis window size $r \times s = 5 \times 3$. All results are percentages.

N_S	N		
	16	20	24
4	27.5	33.7	45.6
6	**23.2**	24.1	29.3
8	41.4	26.6	25.3

Table 3.11 IAMDB WER of the basic off-line HTR system for different values of the number of HMM states N_S and the vertical dimension N, fixing the aspect ratio factor $\rho = 1$ and the analysis window size $r \times s = 5 \times 5$. All results are percentages.

N_S	N		
	16	20	24
4	35.3	34.2	40.6
6	29.4	**25.3**	26.5
8	41.0	25.9	25.8

pora studied in this section.

Results with character language models As previously mentioned, the order of the character n-grams has to be high enough to capture both lexical and syntactical information. Here, we carry out experiments in order to optimize this n-gram order.

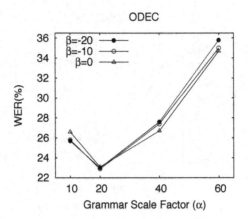

Fig. 3.12   ODEC WER for different values of the grammar scale factor α and word insertion penalty β.

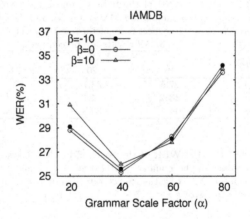

Fig. 3.13   IAMDB WER for different values of the grammar scale factor α and word insertion penalty β.

To carry out the experiments with character language models we have used the HMMs that provides the best results in the previous section. Then, the meta-parameters α and β were tuned for each n-gram order. Table 3.13 shows the best results (CER) obtained for each n-gram order after tuning α and β. The column WLM (Word Language Model) corresponds to the CER computed for the best word-level transcriptions obtained previously.

Table 3.14 is analogous to the Table 3.13. However, in this case the

Table 3.12 WER of the basic off-line HTR system for different corpora. All results are percentages.

CS-page	CS-book	ODEC	IAMDB
28.5	**33.5**	**22.9**	**25.3**

Table 3.13 CER obtained with different character n-grams. All results are percentages.

Corpora	character n-gram order								WLM
	2	3	4	5	6	7	8	9	
ODEC	31.7	26.6	22.6	21.4	**21.4**	21.7	21.8	22.1	12.8
IAM-sentences	37.4	32.0	27.6	25.2	**24.3**	24.5	24.6	24.6	14.8
CS-page	33.1	29.6	27.2	25.7	25.7	**25.5**	25.6	25.6	15.4
CS-book	29.7	26.5	24.3	23.7	23.8	**23.8**	23.9	23.9	18.2

results are shown at the word level, i.e the best WER obtained using character language models for each n-gram order after tuning the α and β are shown.

Table 3.14 WER obtained with different n-grams at character level. All results are percentages.

Corpora	n-gram order								WLM
	2	3	4	5	6	7	8	9	
ODEC	64.4	60.9	49.8	46.7	46.7	**46.6**	46.9	47.6	22.9
IAM-sentences	85.6	68.6	55.6	47.8	**46.2**	46.3	46.9	46.9	25.3
CS-page	72.8	63.0	51.1	50.8	51.0	**50.9**	51.0	51.1	28.5
CS-book	67.7	59.3	51.7	49.6	49.8	**49.6**	49.9	50.2	33.5

As expected, the order of character n-grams which obtain the best results is $n = 6$ or $n = 7$, which is just slightly higher than the average word length.

Results using word language models are significantly better than using language models at character level. This is probably due to the fact that the word language model, along with the corresponding exact and explicit lexicon models, provide better information about how characters and words must be concatenated to obtain correct sentences. In addition, we should recall that the experiments presented here are carried out under the closed-vocabulary assumption. As discussed in section 3.2.3, under this assumption, character n-grams are not expected to exhibit any advantage over the conventional word n-grams.

3.3   On-line Handwritten Text Recognition

The on-line HTR recognizer presented in this section, is used in Chap. 5 to help decoding the feedback touchscreen data for multimodal text corrections in the MM-CATTI system; i.e. to recognize the pen strokes (words) written by the user in successive CATTI interactions in order to amend the errors produced by the main, off-line HTR decoder. In general, touchscreen data consists of a series of pen-positions (x_t, y_t), sampled at regular time instants $t = 1, 2, \ldots$ Each sample of this *"trajectory"* can be accompanied by information about the pen pressure, or by one bit indicating whether the pen is actually touching the screen or not. In this work no pressure information is used. The conceptual architecture adopted for the on-line HTR system is analogous to that used in the off-line HTR system, with exception of the preprocessing and feature extraction modules, which are explained hereafter.

3.3.1   *Preprocessing*

An overview of preprocessing techniques for on-line HTR can be seen in [Huang *et al.* (2007)]. In this work, the preprocessing of each trajectory involves only two simple steps: repeated points elimination and noise reduction.

Repeated points elimination: Repeated points appear in a trajectory when the pen remains down and motionless for some time. These uninformative data are trivially removed, along with the points marked as *"pen-up"*.

Noise reduction: Noise in pen strokes is due to erratic hand motion and inaccuracy of the digitalization process. To reduce this kind of noise, a simple smoothing technique is used which replaces every point (x_t, y_t) in the trajectory by the mean value of its neighbours [Jaeger *et al.* (2001)].

Note that the temporal order of the data points is preserved throughout these preprocessing steps.

3.3.2   *Feature Extraction*

Each preprocessed trajectory is transformed into a new temporal sequence of 6-dimensional real-valued feature vectors [Tosellli *et al.* (2007); Pastor *et al.* (2005a)]. The horizontal coordinate, x, is not directly used as a feature because the x range for different instances of the same character can vary greatly depending on the position of the character into a word. The six features computed for each sample point are:

Normalized Vertical Position y_t: the coordinate pairs of each trajectory point are linearly scaled and translated to obtain new y_t values in the range $[0, 100]$, preserving the original aspect-ratio of the trajectory.

Normalized First Derivatives: x'_t and y'_t are calculated using the method given in [Young *et al.* (1997)]:

$$x'_t = \frac{\Delta x_t}{\sqrt{\Delta x_t^2 + \Delta y_t^2}} \qquad y'_t = \frac{\Delta y_t}{\sqrt{\Delta x_t^2 + \Delta y_t^2}} \qquad (3.7)$$

where,

$$\Delta x_t = \sum_{i=1}^{r} i \cdot (x_{t+i} - x_{t-i}) \qquad \Delta y_t = \sum_{i=1}^{r} i \cdot (y_{t+i} - y_{t-i})$$

The summations upper limit, r, defines a window of size $2r + 1$ which determines the neighbour points involved in the computation. Setting $r = 2$ has provided satisfactory results in this work.

It is worth noting that the normalization of the derivatives by $\sqrt{\Delta x_t^2 + \Delta y_t^2}$ implicitly entails an effective *writing speed normalization*. In our experiments, this has proved to lead to better results than using explicit speed normalization preprocessing techniques such as *trace segmentation*, based on re-sampling the trajectory at equal-length (rather than equal time) intervals [Pastor *et al.* (2005b); Vuori *et al.* (2001)].

Second derivatives: x''_t and y''_t, are computed in the same way as the first derivatives, but using x'_t and y'_t instead of x_t and y_t.

Curvature: k_t, is the inverse of the local radius of the trajectory in each point. It is calculated as:

$$k_t = \frac{x'_t \cdot y''_t - x''_t \cdot y'_t}{\left(x_t'^2 + y_t'^2\right)^{3/2}} \qquad (3.8)$$

Although this feature may be considered redundant because it is an explicit combination of the previous features, it has lead to slightly but consistently improved results in our experiments.

3.3.3   *Recognition*

Modelling and search for on-line recognition follows essentially the same schemes used in off-line recognition, described in Sec. 3.2.3.

As in the off-line case, we use left-to-right continuous density character HMMs with a mixture of Gaussian densities assigned to each state. However, instead of using a fixed number of states for all HMMs, in this case it is variable for each character class. The number of states N_{Sc} chosen for each HMM character class M_c was computed as $N_{Sc} = l_c/f$, where l_c is the average length of the sequences of feature vectors used to train M_c, and f is a design meta-parameter measuring the average number of feature vectors modelled per state (*state load factor*). This rule of setting up N_{Sc} tries to balance modelling effort across states. On the other hand, lexical modelling is carried out in exactly the same way as in the off-line HTR case.

Language modelling and search are simpler in this case because, as we will see in Sec. 5.4, we restrict our MM-CATTI study to single whole-word touchscreen corrections. That is, the language models used in the MM-CATTI search only allow one word per user-interaction.

3.3.4   *Experimental Framework*

In this section the experimental framework adopted to assess the accuracy of the on-line HTR recognizer presented above is described. The corpus used in the experiments, the assessment measures and the meta-parameters to test are defined.

Corpora   The experiments carried out in order to test the effectiveness of the on-line HTR recognizer studied here use the on-line UNIPEN corpus presented in the Sec. 2.5. As previously discussed, the on-line handwritten words needed to assess the performance of the on-line HTR feedback subsystem used on the MM-CATTI system (see Chap. 5) were generated by concatenating random character instances from three UNIPEN categories: digits, lowercase letters and symbols.

In order to tune the meta-parameters of the 68 on-line character HMMs needed, experiments were carried out on each of the 1a, 1c and 1d UNIPEN categories, partitioned into the training and test sets shown in the Table 2.6.

Assessment Measures   Since only single-character classification is considered, the conventional classification error rate (ER) will be used to assess the accuracy of the on-line HTR system. The ER is computed by comparing the character proposed by the system with the reference character, computing the percentage of characters misclassified.

Meta-parameters Two meta-parameters must be adjusted in order to design an accurate recognizer. These parameters are the number of Gaussian densities and the *state load factor* (f) that determines the average number of feature vectors modelled per state.

3.3.5 *Results*

Different experiments have been carried out to assess the basic performance of the on-line HTR recognizer presented here.

All the samples were preprocessed using the preprocessing and feature extraction methods outlined in Sec. 3.3.1 and Sec. 3.3.2. The optimal number of Gaussian densities obtained for the character HMM state mixtures was 16. On the other hand, the *state load factor* (f) that best results obtained was $f = 10$.

The classification error rates (ER) obtained for digits, letters and symbols were 1.7%, 5.9% and 21.8%, respectively. These results are comparable with those of the state-of-the-art results obtained for this dataset. For example in [Ahmad *et al.* (2004)] classification error rates (ER) of 1.5% and 6% are reported for isolated digits and letters, respectively, by using Support Vector Machine. Moreover in [Parizeau *et al.* (2001)], employing neural networks, ER of 3% and 14% for digits and letters are reported. Finally in [Ratzlaff (2003)], an on-line scanning n-tuple classifier system is used for classifying isolated digits, letters and symbols, obtaining in this case ER of 1.1%, 7.6% and 20.4% respectively.

3.4 Summary and Conclusions

In this chapter, an explanation of both basic off- and on-line HTR recognizers to be embedded in the multimodal interactive HTR system described in Chapters 4 and 5 was given in some detail. Both recognizers are based on Hidden Markov Models and n-grams. The HMMs developed have a hierarchical structure with character models at the lowest level. These models are concatenated into words and into whole sentences. To incorporate linguistic information using n-grams, two different approaches have been studied. The first one uses n-grams at word level, whereas in the second one the *n*-grams are used at character level. From the results, we can conclude that using *n*-grams at word level is preferable. On the other hand, given that only single-character classification is considered in this chapter for the on-line recognizer, the language model used is an uni-gram at character level.

Several experiment have been carried out tuning the values of the studied meta-parameters (Sec. 3.2.5). However, it is important to note that, the focus of this chapter is not only about obtaining optimal values of these meta-parameters, but about studying the sensitivity of the recognizers accuracy by varying the values adopted by them. One should bear in mind that the number of meta-parameters under discussion is totally negligible as compared with the overall number of model parameters (millions of N-gram, Gaussian, and state-transition parameters) which, are trained using only the training partitions; for instance in the ODEC database the overall number of HMM and bi-gram parameters is around 1.5 million.

The obtained results are considered as a baseline for the Computer Assisted Transcription of Text Images (CATTI) system and for the Multimodal CATTI (MM-CATTI) system that will be studied in the next chapters.

Chapter 4

Computer Assisted Transcription of Handwritten Text Images

4.1 Introduction

In this chapter the application of the interactive pattern recognition (IPR) framework outlined in Sec. 1.3.3 to the transcription of handwritten documents is discussed. This application is called *Computer Assisted Transcription of Text Images* (CATTI) [Toselli *et al.* (2010, 2007); Romero *et al.* (2007c)]. Rather than full automation, it assists humans in the proper recognition-transcription process; that is, facilitates and speeds up their task of transcription of handwritten texts. The new interactive framework, combines the efficiency of the automatic handwriting recognition system with the accuracy of the human transcriber, integrating the human activity into the recognition process and taking advantage of the user's feedback.

Figure 4.1 shows a schematic view of these ideas. Note that the CATTI system follows the same architecture used on the Chap. 3, composed of four modules: preprocessing, feature extraction, training and recognition. The main difference is that the recognition module used here is adapted to cope with the user feedback. Now, by observing the handwritten text image and the transcription hypothesis that the system derives from the image, the human transcriber is expected to provide some feedback, which may interactively help the system to refine or to improve its hypothesis until it is finally accepted.

We assume that the user provides feedback only to the recognition module. However, a more general user interaction approach would not necessarily be restricted only to this module. The user could interact directly with the preprocessing module in order to correct segmentation or preprocessing errors and the system could take into account these corrections to

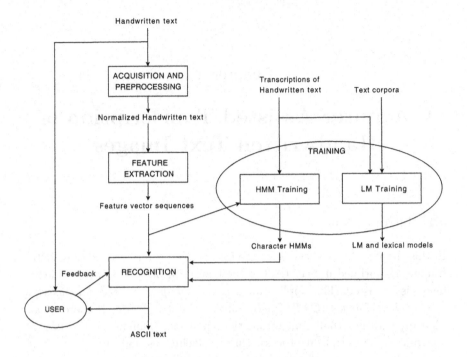

Fig. 4.1   Overview of the CATTI system.

improve the overall recognition accuracy. Nevertheless, in this work, we do not explore these forms of interactivity. The detection and segmentation of text lines from each page has been carried out in a semi-supervised way, and we assume the preprocessing results are error-free.

The CATTI process starts when the HTR system proposes a full transcription $\hat{s}$ of a feature vector sequence $\mathbf{x}$, extracted from a handwritten text image (see Sec. 3.2). Then, the human transcriber (named user from now on) reads this transcription until he or she finds a mistake; i.e, he or she validates a prefix $\mathbf{p}'$ of the transcription which is error-free. Now, the user can enter a word, v, to correct the erroneous text that follows the validated prefix. This action produces a new prefix $\mathbf{p}$ (the previously validated prefix, $\mathbf{p}'$, plus the amendments introduced by the user, v). Then, the system takes into account the new prefix to suggest a suitable continuation to this prefix (i.e., a new $\hat{s}$), thereby starting a new cycle. This process is repeated until a correct, full transcription $\mathbf{T}$ of $\mathbf{x}$ is accepted by the user.

An example of this process is shown in Fig. 4.2. It is worth noting in this example that the WER of the first full transcription hypothesis is

6/7 (85%) and non-interactive post-editing would have required the user to correct *six* errors from the original recognized hypothesis whereas, with the interaction feedback, only *two* user-corrections (the italic and underlined text in the final transcription **T**) are necessary to get the final error-free transcription.

	x	*only*	*one*	*among*	*thousands*	*who*	*do*	*not.*
INTER-0	**p**							
INTER-1	**ŝ ≡ ŵ**	only	our	owing	thousand	letters	to	net
	p'	only						
	v		one					
	p	only	one					
INTER-2	**ŝ**			among	thousands	letters	to	net
	p'	only	one	among	thousands			
	v					who		
	p	only	one	among	thousands	who		
FINAL	**ŝ**						do	not
	v							#
	p ≡ T	only	*one*	among	thousands	*who*	do	not

Fig. 4.2   Example of CATTI interaction to transcribe an image of the English sentence *"only one among thousands who do not"*. Initially the prefix **p** is empty, and the system proposes a complete transcription **ŝ ≡ ŵ** of the input image **x**. In each interaction step the user reads this transcription, accepting a prefix **p'** of it. Then, he or she types in some word, v, to correct the erroneous text that follows the validated prefix, thereby generating a new prefix **p** (the accepted one **p'** plus the word v added by the user). At this point, the system suggests a suitable continuation **ŝ** of this prefix **p** and this process is repeated until a complete and correct transcription of the input signal is reached. In the final transcription, **T**, the underlined italic words are the words typed by the user. In this example the estimated post-editing effort (WER) is 6/7 (85%), while the corresponding interactive estimate (WSR) is 2/7 (29%). This results in an estimated effort reduction (EFR) of 59% (see Sec. 4.7.1 for definitions of WER, WSR and EFR).

In the next sections (4.2-4.4), the formal framework of CATTI will be presented and some modifications to make the system more ergonomic and friendlier to the user will be explained in Sections 4.5 and 4.6. Then, experiments and results are reported in Sec. 4.7. Finally, conclusions are drawn in Sec. 4.9

4.2   Formal Framework

Formally, the CATTI framework can be seen as an instantiation of the problem formulated in Eq. 1.7 where, in addition to the given image **x**, a user-validated *prefix* **p** of the transcription is available. This prefix, which corresponds to the pair (h', d) in Eq. 1.7, contains information from the previous system's prediction (h') plus user's actions, in the form of amendment keystrokes (d). Most specifically, the deterministic feedback, (d), consists of keystrokes or mouse actions to specify a position c in h' where the last correct word appears (validating in this way the longest prefix which is error free, $\mathbf{p}' = h_1'^c$), and a word v to fix the first word error, generating a new prefix, $\mathbf{p} = \mathbf{p}'v$. The HTR system should try to complete this prefix by searching for the most likely *suffix* $\hat{\mathbf{s}}$ ($\hat{h}$ in Eq. (1.7)), according to:

$$\hat{\mathbf{s}} = \operatorname*{argmax}_{\mathbf{s}} \Pr(\mathbf{s} \mid \mathbf{x}, \mathbf{p}) = \operatorname*{argmax}_{\mathbf{s}} \Pr(\mathbf{x} \mid \mathbf{p}, \mathbf{s}) \cdot \Pr(\mathbf{s} \mid \mathbf{p})$$

$$\approx \operatorname*{argmax}_{\mathbf{s}} P(\mathbf{x} \mid \mathbf{p}, \mathbf{s}) \cdot P(\mathbf{s} \mid \mathbf{p}) \qquad (4.1)$$

If the concatenation of $\mathbf{p}$ and $\mathbf{s}$ is denoted as $\mathbf{w}$, equation (4.1) becomes very similar to (3.3). The main difference is that now $\mathbf{p}$ is given. Therefore, the search must be performed over all possible suffixes $\mathbf{s}$ of $\mathbf{p}$ and the language model probability $P(\mathbf{s} \mid \mathbf{p})$ must account for the words that can be written after the prefix $\mathbf{p}$.

In order to solve Eq. (4.1), the signal $\mathbf{x}$ can be considered split into two fragments, $\mathbf{x}_1^b$ and $\mathbf{x}_{b+1}^M$, where M is the length of $\mathbf{x}$. By further considering the boundary point b as a hidden variable in Eq. (4.1), we can write:

$$\hat{\mathbf{s}} \approx \operatorname*{argmax}_{\mathbf{s}} \sum_{1 \leq b \leq M} P(\mathbf{x}, b \mid \mathbf{p}, \mathbf{s}) \cdot P(\mathbf{s} \mid \mathbf{p})$$

$$= \operatorname*{argmax}_{\mathbf{s}} \sum_{1 \leq b \leq M} P(\mathbf{x}_1^b, \mathbf{x}_{b+1}^M \mid \mathbf{p}, \mathbf{s}) \cdot P(\mathbf{s} \mid \mathbf{p}) \qquad (4.2)$$

We can now make the naive (but realistic) assumption that $\mathbf{x}_1^b$ does not depend on the suffix and $\mathbf{x}_{b+1}^M$ does not depend on the prefix, to rewrite Eq. (4.2) as:

$$\hat{\mathbf{s}} \approx \operatorname*{argmax}_{\mathbf{s}} \sum_{1 \leq b \leq M} P(\mathbf{x}_1^b \mid \mathbf{p}) \cdot P(\mathbf{x}_{b+1}^M \mid \mathbf{s}) \cdot P(\mathbf{s} \mid \mathbf{p}) \qquad (4.3)$$

Finally, the sum over all the possible segmentations can be approximated by the dominating term, leading to:

$$\hat{\mathbf{s}} \approx \operatorname*{argmax}_{\mathbf{s}} \max_{1 \leq b \leq M} P(\mathbf{x}_1^b \mid \mathbf{p}) \cdot P(\mathbf{x}_{b+1}^M \mid \mathbf{s}) \cdot P(\mathbf{s} \mid \mathbf{p}) \qquad (4.4)$$

This optimization problem entails finding an optimal boundary point, $\hat{b}$, associated with the optimal suffix decoding, $\hat{\mathbf{s}}$. That is, the signal $\mathbf{x}$ is actually split into two segments, $\mathbf{x}_p = \mathbf{x}_1^{\hat{b}}$ and $\mathbf{x}_s = \mathbf{x}_{\hat{b}+1}^m$. Therefore, the search for the best transcription suffix that completes a prefix $\mathbf{p}$ can be performed just over segments of the signal corresponding to the possible suffixes. On the other hand, as in Eq. 3.3, $P(\mathbf{x}_1^b \mid \mathbf{p})$ and $P(\mathbf{x}_{b+1}^M \mid \mathbf{s})$ can be modelled by HMMs and we can take advantage of the information coming from the prefix to tune the language model constraints modelled by $P(\mathbf{s} \mid \mathbf{p})$.

4.3 Adapting the Language Model

Perhaps the simplest way to deal with $P(\mathbf{s} \mid \mathbf{p})$ is to adapt an n-gram language model to cope with the consolidated prefix. Given that a conventional n-gram models the probability $P(\mathbf{w})$ (where $\mathbf{w}$ is the concatenation of $\mathbf{p}$ and $\mathbf{s}$, i.e the whole sentence), it is necessary to modify this model to take into account the conditional probability $P(\mathbf{s} \mid \mathbf{p})$.

As discussed in [Rodríguez *et al.* (2007)], let $\mathbf{p} = \mathbf{p}_1^k = \mathbf{w}_1^k$ be a consolidated prefix and $\mathbf{s} = \mathbf{s}_1^{l-k} = \mathbf{w}_{k+1}^l$ be a possible suffix. We can compute $P(\mathbf{s} \mid \mathbf{p})$ as:

$$
\begin{aligned}
P(\mathbf{s} \mid \mathbf{p}) &= \frac{P(\mathbf{p}, \mathbf{s})}{P(\mathbf{p})} \\
&= \frac{\prod_{i=1}^{l} P(w_i \mid \mathbf{w}_{i-n+1}^{i-1})}{\prod_{i=1}^{k} P(w_i \mid \mathbf{w}_{i-n+1}^{i-1})} \\
&= \prod_{i=k+1}^{l} P(w_i \mid \mathbf{w}_{i-n+1}^{i-1})
\end{aligned}
\tag{4.5}
$$

Moreover, for the terms from $k+1$ to $k+n-1$ of this factorization, we have additional information coming from the already known words $\mathbf{w}_{k-n+2}^{k}$, allowing us to decompose Eq. (4.5) as:

$$
\begin{aligned}
P(\mathbf{s} \mid \mathbf{p}) &= \prod_{i=k+1}^{k+n-1} P(w_i \mid \mathbf{w}_{i-n+1}^{i-1}) \cdot \prod_{i=k+n}^{l} P(w_i \mid \mathbf{w}_{i-n+1}^{i-1}) \\
&= \prod_{j=1}^{n-1} P(s_j \mid \mathbf{p}_{k-n+1+j}^{k}, \mathbf{s}_1^{j-1}) \cdot \prod_{j=n}^{l-k} P(s_j \mid \mathbf{s}_{j-n+1}^{j-1})
\end{aligned}
\tag{4.6}
$$

The first term of Eq. (4.6) accounts for the probability of the $n-1$ words of the suffix, whose probability is conditioned by words from the validated prefix, and the second one is the usual n-gram probability for the rest of the words in the suffix.

4.4   Searching

In the first iteration of the CATTI process, **p** is empty. Therefore, the HTR recognizer has to generate a full transcription of **x** as shown in Eq. (3.3). Afterwards, the user-validated prefix **p** has to be used to generate a suitable continuation **s** in the following interactions of the interactive transcription process.

We can explicitly rely on Eq. (4.4) to implement a decoding process in one step, as in conventional HTR systems. The decoder should be forced to *match* the previously validated prefix **p** and then continue searching for a suffix **ŝ** according to the constraints (4.6) [Rodríguez *et al.* (2007)].

In this section, two possible implementations of the CATTI decoder are described. The first one is based on the well known Viterbi algorithm [Jelinek (1998)], and the other in word-graph techniques (see Chap. 1) similar to those described in [Barrachina *et al.* (2009)] for Computer Assisted Translation and in [Liu and Soong (2006)] for multimodal speech post-editing. The computational cost of the second approach is much lower than using the naïve Viterbi adaptation, at the expense of a moderate accuracy degradation. Using word-graph techniques makes it possible to actually interact with the human transcribers in a time-efficient way.

4.4.1   *Direct Viterbi-based Approach*

The search problem corresponding to Eq. (4.4) and Eq. (4.6) can be solved by dynamically building special language models, each of which can be seen as the "concatenation" of a *linear* model which strictly accounts for the successive words in **p** and the "suffix language model" of Eq. (4.6). First, an *n*-gram is built from the available training set. Then, at each interaction step, a linear model which accounts for the validated prefix is constructed, and these two models are combined into a single model. An example of this combination is shown in the Fig. 4.3.

Owing to the finite-state nature of these special language models, the search involved in Eq. (4.4) can be efficiently carried out using the Viterbi algorithm. Apart from the optimal suffix decoding, **ŝ**, a correspondingly optimal segmentation of the **x** is then obtained as a byproduct.

Training samples (L)

only one among thousands

only among thousands

only one coming soon

mainly thousands

only soon

only one thing among

only among thousands

only are coming thousands

only are coming soon

Prefix (L_P) = only one

Original Bigram (L)

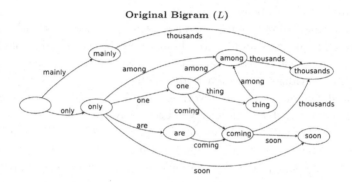

Model for the Prefix (L_p)

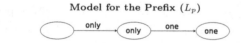

Final Combined Model ($L_p L_s$)

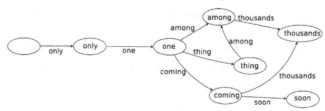

Fig. 4.3 Example of a CATTI dynamic language model building. First, an n-gram (L) for the training set of the figure is built. Then, a linear model (L_p) which accounts for the prefix "*only one*" is constructed. Finally, these two models are combined into a single model as shown in ($L_p L_s$).

4.4.2　Word-graph based Approach

It should be noted that the direct adaptation of the Viterbi algorithm, explained in the previous section, to implement these techniques lead to a computational cost that grows quadratically with the number of words of each sentence. This is because, at each user interaction, a Viterbi search must be carried out. So, although pruning techniques such as beam search can be used, the process can become prohibitively slow. This can be problematic for large sentences and/or for fine grained (character-level) interaction schemes. Nevertheless, using word-graph techniques, very efficient, linear cost search can be easily achieved.

In this case, we only have to construct a word-graph for each line or sentence (this process can be carried out in batch mode) and then all the computations needed at each interactive step can be very efficiently carried out on this previously computed word-graph.

As explained in Sec. 1.3.4, a word graph (WG) is a data structure that represents a set of strings in a very efficient way. In handwritten recognition, a WG represents a large amount of sequences of words whose posterior probability $\Pr(\mathbf{w} \mid \mathbf{x})$ is large enough, according to the morphological (likelihood) and language (prior) models used to decode a text image, represented as a sequence of feature vectors. In other words, the word graph is just (a pruned version of) the Viterbi search trellis obtained when transcribing the whole image sentence. Since the size of the full trellis is prohibitive, we use the position synchronous pruning strategy, where at each state only the most promising hypotheses are retained. The number of possible transcriptions depends of the word graph density (WGD). It is defined, for a handwritten sentence, as the total number of word graph edges divided by the number of actually written words in the text image represented by the WG [Ortmanns et al. (1997)].

As discussed in Sec. 1.3.4, in Eqs. 1.11-1.15, the probability of a word subsequence, $\mathbf{w}$, in a word-graph is approximated as the maximum of the probabilities of all the paths that generate $\mathbf{w}$, $\sigma(\mathbf{w})$:

$$P(\mathbf{w}) \approx \max_{\phi_\mathbf{w} \in d(\mathbf{w})} P(\phi_\mathbf{w}) = \max_{\phi_\mathbf{w} \in \sigma(\mathbf{w})} \prod_{k=1}^{l} P(\phi_\mathbf{w}) \qquad (4.7)$$

where $\phi_\mathbf{w} = \{e_1 = (z_0, z_1), e_2 = (z_1, z_2), ..., e_l = (z_{l-1}, z_l)\}$ is a sequence of edges such that $\mathbf{w} = \omega(e_1)\omega(e_2)...\omega(e_l)$. We say that $\mathbf{w}$ is a complete word sequence if the paths associated to it are complete paths; that is, z_0 is the initial WG node n_I, and z_l is one of the final WG nodes, i.e., $z_l \in F$, and its probability is analogous to the previous one, but considering only the set of complete paths, $f(\mathbf{w})$, associated with $\mathbf{w}$.

The probability of an edge, $e_k = (z_{k-1}, z_k)$, in a WG is the product of the morphological-lexical probability, $P_M(\cdot)$, of the image elements between its start and end node points, $\mathbf{x}_{t(z_{k-1})+1}^{t(z_k)}$, times the language model probability, $P_L(\cdot)$, of the given word at the edge $\omega(e_k)$. That is,

$$p(e_k) = P(\mathbf{x}_{t(z_{k-1})+1}^{t(z_k)} \mid \omega(e_k)) \cdot P(\omega(e_k)) \tag{4.8}$$

So, the word subsequence probability can be written as:

$$P(\mathbf{w}) \approx \max_{\phi_\mathbf{w} \in \sigma(\mathbf{w})} \prod_{k=1}^{l} P(\mathbf{x}_{t(z_{k-1})+1}^{t(z_k)} \mid \omega(e_k)) \cdot P(\omega(e_k)) \tag{4.9}$$

Given a WG, the complete word sequence with greatest probability is approximated as:

$$\hat{\mathbf{w}} \approx \operatorname*{argmax}_{\mathbf{w}} \max_{\phi_\mathbf{w} \in f(\mathbf{w})} \prod_{k=1}^{l} P(\mathbf{x}_{t(z_{k-1})+1}^{t(z_k)} \mid \omega(e_k)) \cdot P(\omega(e_k)) \tag{4.10}$$

which can be efficiently computed by means of the Viterbi search algorithm.

During the CATTI process, first a WG is computed for a given input line or sentence. Then, the system makes use of this WG in order to complete the prefixes accepted by the human transcriber. In other words, the search problem consists in finding the target suffix $\mathbf{s}$ that maximizes the posterior probability given a prefix $\mathbf{p}$ as described in Eq. (4.1).

To solve this problem, first the decoder parses the previously validated prefix $\mathbf{p}$ over the WG. This parsing procedure will end defining a set of end nodes Q_p of the paths, whose associated word sequence is $\mathbf{p}$. Then, departing from any of the nodes in Q_p, the decoder continues searching for a suffix $\mathbf{s}$ that maximizes the posterior probability. Therefore, the boundary point b in Eqs. (4.2)-(4.4) is now restricted to values $t(q) \; \forall q \in Q_p$ and Eq. (4.4) is now approximated as:

$$\hat{\mathbf{s}} = \operatorname*{argmax}_{\mathbf{s}} \max_{q \in Q_p} P(\mathbf{x}_1^{t(q)} \mid p) \cdot P(\mathbf{x}_{t(q)+1}^{M} \mid \mathbf{s}) \cdot P(\mathbf{s} \mid \mathbf{p}) \tag{4.11}$$

The suffix probability, which corresponds with the last two terms of the previous equation, is computed as the probability of a word subsequence (Eq. 4.9), starting in a node from Q_p and ending in a final node. Similarly, the probability of the prefix is computed as the word subsequence probability starting in the initial node, n_I and ending in a node from Q_p.

This search problem can be efficiently carried out using dynamic programming. In order to make the process faster, first, we apply a shortest-path algorithm backwards to compute the best path and its probability from any node to the final node. Note that we only need to carry out this computation once, when the WG is generated. Then, we look for the set of boundary nodes Q_p. Finally, we only have to multiply the probability computed from the initial node to any node $q \in Q_p$ times the (previously computed) probability from q to the final node, and choose the node with maximum product.

An example of a word graph is shown in Fig. 1.5. This word graph represents a set of possible transcriptions of the handwritten sentence "*only one among thousands who do not*". The system uses this WG in the interactive transcription process to obtain a perfect transcription, following the above explained WG search phases. The initial hypothesis is the highest probability word sequence, "*only our owing thousands letters to net*". The user supervise this hypothesis until the first wrong word is detected, which is the word "*our*". After correcting this error, the prefix "*only one*" became fixed. In the first phase, the decoder parses this prefix over the WG finding the set of nodes $Q_p = \{3\}$, which correspond to paths from the initial node whose associated word sequence is "*only one*". Then, the decoder continues searching for the suffix **s** with maxim posterior probability from any of the nodes in Q_p. In this example, the suffix that maximizes the posterior probability is "*among thousands letters to net*". In this new system hypothesis, the wrong words "*owing*" and "*thousand*" are corrected automatically. Then, in a new interaction step, the user corrects the next error, in this case the word "*letters*". Finally, the system uses this new validated prefix to search for the next best prefix-compatible hypothesis in the WG. This yield the word sequence $\mathbf{w}_4$, which is already the correct word sequence. This process is graphically shown in Fig. 4.2.

In order to avoid numeric underflow problems that can appear with small probabilities, log-probabilities are generally used. So, a score $\varphi(e_i)$ is associated to each edge, e, as follows:

$$\varphi(e_i) = \log P(\mathbf{x}_{t(z_{i-1})+1}^{t(z_i)} \mid \omega(e_i)) + \log P(\omega(e_i)) \qquad (4.12)$$

In addition, the simple sum is modified to balance the absolute values of the two log-probabilities involved. The most common modification is to use the *grammar scale factor*, α (GSF), and the *word insertion penalty*, β (WIP), as they are used in Eq. (3.4). So, now the score of each edge is:

$$\varphi(e_i) = \log P(\mathbf{x}_{t(z_{i-1})+1}^{t(z_i)} \mid \omega(e_i)) + \alpha \log P(\omega(e_i)) + \beta \qquad (4.13)$$

This can be properly seen as a log-linear combination of feature functions [Berger *et al.* (1996)]. Note, that Eq. (4.12) and Eq. (4.13) are identical when $\alpha = 1$ and $\beta = 0$.

4.4.2.1 *Error-correction parsing*

The word graph is a representation of a large (but finite) *subset* of the possible transcriptions for a source handwritten text image, where the size of this subset depends of the word graph density. Hence, it may happen that the correct transcription of a handwritten sentence is not found in this subset. This implies that some prefixes given by the user may not be exactly found in the word graph. For example, 16% of the words of the CS corpus (see Chap.2) validated by the user are not included in the corresponding word-graphs. In the IAMDB and ODEC these values are around 7% and 8%, respectively.

A solution is not to use $\mathbf{p}$ itself but, among all the possible prefixes in the word graph, look for a prefix $\mathbf{p}_e$ that best matches the given prefix. By considering this prefix as a hidden variable, the problem of searching for the most likely suffix $\mathbf{s}$ given $\mathbf{p}$ can be formulated as:

$$
\hat{\mathbf{s}} \approx \operatorname*{argmax}_{\mathbf{s}} P(\mathbf{s} \mid \mathbf{x}, \mathbf{p})
$$

$$
= \operatorname*{argmax}_{\mathbf{s}} \sum_{\mathbf{p}_e} P(\mathbf{s}, \mathbf{p}_e \mid \mathbf{x}, \mathbf{p})
$$

$$
= \operatorname*{argmax}_{\mathbf{s}} \sum_{\mathbf{p}_e} P(\mathbf{x} \mid \mathbf{p}, \mathbf{p}_e, \mathbf{s}) \cdot P(\mathbf{p}_e, \mathbf{s} \mid \mathbf{p})
$$

$$
= \operatorname*{argmax}_{\mathbf{s}} \sum_{\mathbf{p}_e} P(\mathbf{x} \mid \mathbf{p}, \mathbf{p}_e, \mathbf{s}) \cdot P(\mathbf{s} \mid \mathbf{p}, \mathbf{p}_e) \cdot P(\mathbf{p}_e \mid \mathbf{p})
$$

$$(4.14)$$

We can make the naive assumption that $P(\mathbf{x} \mid \mathbf{p}, \mathbf{p}_e, \mathbf{s})$ and $P(\mathbf{s} \mid \mathbf{p}, \mathbf{p}_e)$ do not depend of $\mathbf{p}$ given $\mathbf{p}_e$ and $\mathbf{s}$ to rewrite Eq. (4.14) as:

$$
\hat{\mathbf{s}} \approx \operatorname*{argmax}_{\mathbf{s}} \sum_{\mathbf{p}_e} P(\mathbf{x} \mid \mathbf{p}_e, \mathbf{s}) \cdot P(\mathbf{s} \mid \mathbf{p}_e) \cdot P(\mathbf{p}_e \mid \mathbf{p}) \qquad (4.15)
$$

Taking now into account the boundary nodes, as in Eq. (4.11):

$$
\hat{\mathbf{s}} \approx \operatorname*{argmax}_{\mathbf{s}} \sum_{\mathbf{p}_e} \sum_{q \in Q} P(\mathbf{x}, q \mid \mathbf{p}_e, \mathbf{s}) \cdot P(\mathbf{s} \mid \mathbf{p}_e) \cdot P(\mathbf{p}_e \mid \mathbf{p}) \qquad (4.16)
$$

and following similar assumptions as in Eq. (4.3) and Eq. (4.4) we can rewrite the previous equation as:

$$\hat{s} \approx \operatorname*{argmax}_{s} \max_{\mathbf{p}_e} \max_{q \in Q} P(\mathbf{x}_1^{t(q)} \mid \mathbf{p}_e) \cdot P(\mathbf{x}_{t(q)+1}^M \mid \mathbf{s}) \cdot P(\mathbf{s} \mid \mathbf{p}_e) \cdot P(\mathbf{p}_e \mid \mathbf{p})$$

$$(4.17)$$

where $P(\mathbf{p}_e \mid \mathbf{p})$ models a probability distribution of similarity between $\mathbf{p}_e$ and $\mathbf{p}$.

$P(\mathbf{p}_e \mid \mathbf{p})$ can be implemented in terms of probabilistic error correcting parsing. This can be easily done by expanding the WG with a set of edges that represent the different editing operations. In Fig. 4.4 we can see an example of all the added edges between two nodes [Amengual and Vidal (1998)].

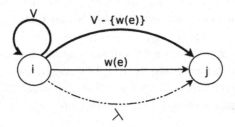

Fig. 4.4   Example of edges added to a WG between the nodes i and j for probabilistic error correcting parsing. The edge labelled with the word $\omega(e)$ is the original edge and corresponds to the operation of replacing the word $\omega(e)$ with itself. The group of edges labelled with $V - \{\omega(e)\}$ represent the substitution of $\omega(e)$ for another word. Here we have an edge for each word in the vocabulary with exception of $\omega(e)$. The edge labelled with λ (empty symbol) models a deletion. Finally, the last group is for insertions, involving an edge for each word in the vocabulary from a state to itself.

Until now, an edge has been defined by its start and end nodes. However this is not longer possible due to the fact that now there is more than one edge between two adjacent nodes. For this reason, each edge must now be defined by its start and end nodes, and a word related with this edge: $e' = (i, j, v)$. As with the original edge, its probability is modelled as a log-linear combination. A new term is added to model the similarity between the original edge and the new edge. It is given by[1] $-l(v, v')$, where[2] $v' \in V \cup \{\lambda\}$ and $l(v, v')$ is the Levenstein distance between v and

---

[1]That is, $\log \exp^{-l(v,v')}$, which corresponds to the popular assumption that the probability of changing v' into v decreases exponentially with the Levenstein distance between v and v'.

[2]The symbol λ represents the empty word.

v'. Therefore, the score of an expanded edge is computed as:

$$\varphi(i,j,v) = \begin{cases} \log P(\mathbf{x}_{t(i)+1}^{t(j)} \mid \omega(e)) + \alpha \log P(\omega(e)) + \beta - \gamma l(\omega(e), v) \\ \qquad\qquad\qquad\qquad\qquad\qquad\qquad i \neq j, e = (i,j) \\ \\ \beta - \gamma l(\lambda, v) \qquad\qquad\qquad\qquad\qquad i = j \end{cases}$$

$$(4.18)$$

where e is the original edge between the nodes i and j and the parameter $\gamma > 0$ weights the penalization due to the number of different characters according to $l(.,.)$. Note that if $\omega(e) = v$, the number of different characters is 0 and Eq. (4.18) and Eq. (4.13) become identical.

Taking into account Eq. 4.18, the computation of Eq 4.17 can be implemented using dynamic programming. The computational effort can be further improved by visiting the WG nodes in topological order [Amengual and Vidal (1998)] and incorporating beam-search techniques [Lowerre (1976)] to discard those nodes whose score is worse than a fraction of the best score at the current stage of the parsing. Moreover, the error-correcting algorithm can take advantage of the incremental nature of $\mathbf{p}$, to parse only the new suffix (typically just one word) of $\mathbf{p}$ provided by the user in the last interaction step.

4.5   Increasing Interaction Ergonomy

In CATTI applications the user is repeatedly interacting with the system. Hence, making the interaction process easy is crucial for the success of the system. In conventional CATTI, before typing a new word in order to correct a hypothesis, the user needs to position the cursor in the place where she wants to type the word. This is done by performing a *Pointer Action* (PA) by means of any kind of pointer-device like a typical mouse for example or by means of "accelerator" keystrokes. By doing so, the user is already providing a very useful information to the system: he/she is validating a prefix up to the position where she positioned the cursor, and, in addition, she is implicitly signalling that the following word located after the cursor is incorrect. Hence, the system can already take advantage of this fact and directly propose a new suitable suffix in which the first word is different from the first wrong word of the previous suffix. This way, many explicit user corrections are avoided [Romero *et al.* (2008, 2009c)].

In Fig. 4.5 we can see an example of the CATTI process with the new interaction mode, which will be referred henceforth as PA-CATTI. As in the conventional CATTI, the process starts when the HTR system proposes a full transcription ŝ of the input image **x**. Then, the user reads this prediction until a transcription error is found (v) and makes a PA (m) to position the cursor at this point. This way, the user validates an error-free transcription prefix **p'**. Now, before the user introduces a word to correct the erroneous one, the HTR system, taking into account the new prefix and the wrong word (v) that follows the validated prefix, suggests a suitable continuation to this prefix (i.e., a new ŝ). If the new ŝ corrects the erroneous word (v) a new cycle starts. Otherwise, if the new ŝ has an error in the same position that the previous one, the user can enter a word, k, to correct the erroneous text v. This action produces a new prefix **p** (the previously validated prefix, **p'**, followed by k). Then, the HTR system takes into account the new prefix to suggest a new suffix and a new cycle starts. This process is repeated until a correct transcription of **x** is accepted by the user.

	x	*only one among thousands who do not.*						
INTER-0	**p**							
	ŝ ≡ ŵ	only	our	owing	thousand	letters	to	net
	m		↑					
	p'	only						
INTER-1	- - - -	- -						
	ŝ		are	owing	thousand	letters	to	net
	k		one					
	p	only	one					
INTER-2	ŝ			among	thousands	letters	to	net
	m					↑		
	p'	only	one	among	thousands			
	ŝ					who	do	not
FINAL	k							not #
	p ≡ **T**	only	*one*	among	thousands	who	do	not

Fig. 4.5 Example of PA-CATTI operation with pointer feedback. Starting with an initial recognized hypothesis ŝ, the user validates its longest well-recognized prefix **p'**, making a pointer-action (m), and the system proposes a new suffix, ŝ. As the new hypothesis does not correct the mistake the user types the correct word k, generating a new validated prefix **p** (k concatenated to **p'**). Taking into account the new prefix the system suggests a new hypothesis ŝ starting a new cycle. Now, the user validates the longest prefix **p'** which is error-free. The system takes into account the new prefix **p'** to propose a new suffix ŝ one more time. As the new hypothesis corrects the erroneous word a new cycle start. This process is repeated until the final error-free transcription **T** is obtained. The underlined italic word in the final transcription is the only word which was corrected by the user. Note that in the interaction step 1, it is needed a pointer "click" to validate the longest prefix that is error-free and then, to type the correct word. However, the interaction step 2 only needs the pointer positioning action.

In the example shown in Fig. 4.5, without interaction, a user should have to correct *six* errors from the original recognized hypothesis. If the conventional CATTI is used, the user only has to correct *two* words. However, with the new PA interaction mode, which somehow tries to anticipate the possible corrections that could be carried out by the user in the conventional CATTI context, only one user-correction is necessary to get the final error-free transcription. Note that in the interaction step 1 a (single) PA does not succeeds and the correct word needs to be physically typed. However, the interaction step 2 only needs a PA.

This new kind of interaction needs not be restricted to single PAs. Several scenarios arise, depending on the number of times the user performs a PA. In the simplest one, the user only makes a PA when it is necessary to displace the cursor. In this case the PA does not involve any extra human effort, because it is the same action that the user should make in the conventional CATTI to position the cursor before typing the correct word. This simple scenario will be called SPA (Single Pointer Action) from now on.

Another scenario that can be considered consists in performing a PA systematically before writing, even in those cases where the cursor is already in the correct position. In this case, however, there is a cost associated to this kind of PAs, since the user does need to perform additional actions, which may or may not be beneficial. This scenario can be easily extended allowing to the user to make several PAs before deciding to make an explicit word correction.

Since we have already dealt, in the Sec. 4.2, with the problem of finding a suitable suffix $\hat{s}$ when the user validates a prefix $\mathbf{p}'$ and introduces a correct word k, we focus now on the problem in which the user only makes a PA. In this case the decoder has to cope with the input image $\mathbf{x}$, the validated prefix $\mathbf{p}'$ and the erroneous word that follows the validated prefix v, in order to search for a transcription suffix $\hat{s}$:

$$\hat{\mathbf{s}} = \operatorname*{argmax}_{s} \Pr(\mathbf{s} \mid \mathbf{x}, \mathbf{p}', v) \approx \operatorname*{argmax}_{s} P(\mathbf{x} \mid \mathbf{p}', \mathbf{s}, v) \cdot P(\mathbf{s} \mid \mathbf{p}', v) \quad (4.19)$$

Similar assumptions and developments as those followed in Sec. 4.2 can be made with $P(\mathbf{x} \mid \mathbf{p}', \mathbf{s}, v)$. On the other hand, $P(\mathbf{s} \mid \mathbf{p}', v)$ can be provided by a language model constrained by the validated prefix $\mathbf{p}'$ and by the erroneous word that follows it.

With respect to the scenario which allows the user to perform several PAs before deciding to write the correct word, the successive corresponding values of v must be cached and $P(\mathbf{s} \mid \mathbf{p}', v)$ must be computed taking into account all the previously discarded values of v (not just the one from the previous step).

4.5.1   *Language Modelling and Search*

$P(\mathbf{s} \mid \mathbf{p'}, v)$ can be approached by adapting an n-gram language model so as to cope with the validated prefix $\mathbf{p'}$ and with the erroneous word that follows it, v. The language model presented in Sec. 4.3 would provide a model for the probability $P(\mathbf{s} \mid \mathbf{p'})$, but now the first word of $\mathbf{s}$ is conditioned by v. Therefore, some changes are needed.

Let $\mathbf{p'} = \mathbf{p'}_1^k = \mathbf{w}_1^k$ be the validated prefix and $\mathbf{s} = \mathbf{s}_1^{l-k} = \mathbf{w}_{k+1}^l$ be a possible suffix. Considering that the wrongly recognized word v only affects the first word of the suffix w_{k+1}, $P(\mathbf{s} \mid \mathbf{p'}, v)$ can be computed as:

$$P(\mathbf{s} \mid \mathbf{p'}, v) \simeq P(w_{k+1} \mid \mathbf{w}_{k+2-n}^k, v) \cdot \prod_{i=k+2}^{k+n-1} P(w_i \mid \mathbf{w}_{i-n+1}^{i-1})$$

$$\cdot \prod_{i=k+n}^{l} P(w_i \mid \mathbf{w}_{i-n+1}^{i-1})$$

$$= P(s_1 \mid \mathbf{p'}_{k+2-n}^k, v) \cdot \prod_{j=2}^{n-1} P(s_j \mid \mathbf{p'}_{k-n+1+j}^k)$$

$$\cdot \prod_{j=n}^{l-k} P(s_j \mid \mathbf{s}_{j-n+1}^{j-1}) \tag{4.20}$$

Now, taking into account that the first word of the possible suffix s_1 has to be different to the erroneous word v, $P(s_1 \mid \mathbf{p'}_{k+2-n}^k, v)$ becomes:

$$P(s_1 \mid \mathbf{p'}_{k+2-n}^k, v) = \frac{\bar{\delta}(s_1, v) \cdot P(s_1 \mid \mathbf{p'}_{k+2-n}^k)}{\sum_{v'} \bar{\delta}(v', v) \cdot P(v' \mid \mathbf{p'}_{k+2-n}^k)} \tag{4.21}$$

where $\bar{\delta}(v, v')$ is 0 when $v = v'$ and 1 otherwise. Since, $\sum_{v'} \bar{\delta}(v', v) \cdot P(v' \mid \mathbf{p'}_{k+2-n}^k)$ is the same for any s_1, we can use just $\bar{\delta}(s_1, v) \cdot P(s_1 \mid \mathbf{p'}_{k+2-n}^k)$ during the search process of $\hat{\mathbf{s}}$ (Eq. (4.19)).

As in the conventional CATTI, the search problem involved in the Eq. (4.19) can be solved by building a special language model, but now the "Suffix Language Model" of the Eq. (4.20) is modified in accordance with Eq. (4.21). Thanks to the finite-state nature of this special language model, the search involved in Eq. (4.19) can be carried out using the Viterbi algorithm.

In the PA-CATTI approach, the system must react immediately by emitting a new suggested suffix after each pointer action performed by the user. Therefore, the response speed becomes a very crucial factor to be taken into account. For this reason, search implementation based on word-graph techniques results the more convenient solution. The restrictions entailed by Eq. 4.21 can be easily implemented by disabling the edge labelled with the word v after the prefix has been matched. An example is shown in Fig. 4.6. This example assumes the user has validated the prefix "only one among thousands" and the wrongly-recognized word was "letters". Hence, the new word-graph has the edge labelled with the word "letters" disabled.

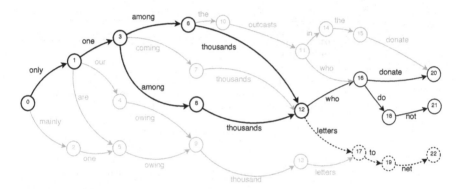

Fig. 4.6 Example of word-graph generated after the user validates the prefix "only one among thousands". The edge corresponding to the wrong-recognized word "letters" was disabled.

4.6 Interacting at the Character Level

Until now, human feedback for CATTI has been assumed to come in the form of whole-word interactions; i.e, the system does not start a new cycle until the user enters a whole-word. This will allow us to properly estimate the user-effort reduction achieved by CATTI with respect to conventional post-editing of automatic transcriptions. Nevertheless, character-level keystroke interactions can allow for more ergonomic and friendly interfaces. In this section this new level of interaction is presented. Now, as soon as the user introduces a new keystroke, the system proposes a new suitable continuation.

In Fig. 4.7 we can see an example of the CATTI process at the character level. As in the conventional CATTI, the process starts when the HTR system proposes a full transcription $\hat{s}$ of the input image $\mathbf{x}$. Then, the user validates the longest prefix that is error free, $\mathbf{p}$', and enters a single keystroke or character, c, to correct the erroneous text that follows the validated prefix, producing a new prefix $\mathbf{p}$. The last word of this new prefix is not necessarily complete. In this case, the system must suggest a suitable continuation whose first part completes the incomplete word validated by the user. This process is repeated until a correct transcription of $\mathbf{x}$ is accepted by the user.

	$\mathbf{x}$	*only*	*one*	*among*	*thousands*	*who*	*do*	*not.*
INTER-0	$\mathbf{p}$							
INTER-1	$\hat{s} \equiv \hat{w}$	only	our	owing	thousand	letters	to	net
	$\mathbf{p}$'	only	o					
	c		n					
	$\mathbf{p}$	only	on					
INTER-2	$\hat{s}$		e	among	thousands	letters	to	net
	$\mathbf{p}$'	only	one	among	thousands			
	c					w		
	$\mathbf{p}$	only	one	among	thousands	w		
FINAL	$\hat{s}$					who	do	not
	c							#
	$\mathbf{p} \equiv \mathbf{T}$	only	o$\underline{n}$e	among	thousands	$\underline{w}$ho	do	not

Fig. 4.7   Example of CATTI operation at character level. Starting with an initial recognized hypothesis $\hat{s}$, the user validates its longest well-recognized prefix $\mathbf{p}$' and corrects the following erroneous character c, generating a new validated prefix $\mathbf{p}$ (c concatenated to $\mathbf{p}$'). This new prefix $\mathbf{p}$ is submitted as additional feedback to the recognition system which, based on this, proposes a new suffix $\hat{s}$. This process goes on until the final error-free transcription $\mathbf{T}$ is obtained. Underlined italic characters in the final transcription are those which were corrected by user.

Two different approaches to develop the character-level keystroke interaction can be considered. The first one consists in using language models at character level. In this case the language model would account for the overall concatenation of characters into text lines or sentences. All the explanation given in previous sections has been made at word level. However, it can be extended to character level by replacing $\mathbf{w}$ with $\mathbf{c}$, where $\mathbf{c}$ is a sequence of characters. However, in Chap. 3 we have carried out experiments using character language models and the obtained results showed that using these language models significantly degrades the accuracy with respect to using language models at word level. So, we have decided not to follow this approach.

In the second approach, we work with language models at word level exactly as we have done previously. In this case, the system looks for the most probable word that begins with the incomplete word that the user has validated. In order to "autocomplete" the last incomplete word of the prefix and propose a suitable continuation, we assume that the prefix $\mathbf{p}$ is divided into two fragments: $\mathbf{p}$" and v_p, where $\mathbf{p}$" is the longest part of the prefix formed by complete words and v_p is the last incomplete word of the prefix. In the example presented in Fig. 4.7, in the first interaction step, INTER-1, $\mathbf{p}$" is "*only*" and v_p is "*on*". In this case the decoder has to cope with the input image $\mathbf{x}$, the validated prefix $\mathbf{p}$" and the incomplete word v_p, in order to search for a best transcription suffix $\hat{\mathbf{s}}$, whose first part is a completion of the incomplete word v_p:

$$\hat{\mathbf{s}} = \underset{\mathbf{s}}{\operatorname{argmax}} \Pr(\mathbf{s} \mid \mathbf{x}, \mathbf{p}", v_p)$$

$$= \underset{\mathbf{s}}{\operatorname{argmax}} \Pr(\mathbf{x} \mid \mathbf{p}", v_p, \mathbf{s}) \cdot \Pr(\mathbf{s} \mid \mathbf{p}", v_p)$$

$$\approx \underset{\mathbf{s}}{\operatorname{argmax}} P(\mathbf{x} \mid \mathbf{p}", v_p, \mathbf{s}) \cdot P(\mathbf{s} \mid \mathbf{p}", v_p) \quad (4.22)$$

Assumptions and developments similar to those followed in Sec. 4.2 can be made here with $P(\mathbf{x} \mid \mathbf{p}", v_p, \mathbf{s})$. On the other hand, $P(\mathbf{s} \mid \mathbf{p}", v_p)$ can be provided by a language model constrained by the part of the prefix formed by complete words, $\mathbf{p}$", and by the incomplete word that follows it, v_p.

4.6.1 *Language Modelling and Search*

To implement $P(\mathbf{s} \mid \mathbf{p}", v_p)$ we assume that the suffix $\mathbf{s}$ is divided into two fragments: v_s and $\mathbf{s}$'. The first fragment, v_s, corresponds to the final part of the incomplete word of the prefix. That is, $v_p v_s = v$ where v is an existing word in the task dictionary. The other fragment, $\mathbf{s}$', is the rest of the suffix. In the example shown in Fig. 4.7, in the interaction step 1, v_s is "e" and $\mathbf{s}$' is "among thousands letters to net". So, the search must be performed over all possible suffixes $\mathbf{s}$ of $\mathbf{p}$, whose first part, v_s, concatenated with the last part of the prefix v_p, form an existing word (v) in the task dictionary. The language model probability $P(v_s, \mathbf{s}' \mid \mathbf{p}", v_p)$ can be decomposed into two terms:

$$P(v_s, \mathbf{s}' \mid \mathbf{p}", v_p) = P(\mathbf{s}' \mid \mathbf{p}", v_p, v_s) \cdot P(v_s \mid \mathbf{p}", v_p) \quad (4.23)$$

The first term accounts for the probability of all the whole words in the suffix, and can be modelled with the language model presented in Sec. 4.3. The second term ensures that the first part of the suffix v_s, will be a possible suffix of the incomplete word v_p. This probability can be written as:

$$P(v_s \mid \mathbf{p}", v_p) = \frac{P(v_p, v_s \mid \mathbf{p}")}{\sum_{v'_s} P(v_p, v'_s \mid \mathbf{p}")} \qquad (4.24)$$

To cope with the higher computational demands entailed by such fine-grained operations, word graphs are used as in the conventional CATTI. The restrictions entailed by the Eq. (4.24) can be easily implemented by disabling the edges labelled with a word that does not begin with v_p after the prefix has been matched. An example is shown in Fig. 4.8. In this example the user has validated the prefix "only on". Hence, in the word-graph, all the edges with a word that does not begin with "on" after matching the prefix are disabled. If no edge is labelled with a word that begins with v_p, the system looks for the word in the word-graph vocabulary and then applies the error-correcting algorithm explained in Sec. 4.4.2. Finally, if no word in the word-graph vocabulary begins with v_p, the system looks for the word in the task vocabulary, applying then the error-correcting algorithm. This process will be called "Character-level CATTI" (CL-CATTI) from now on.

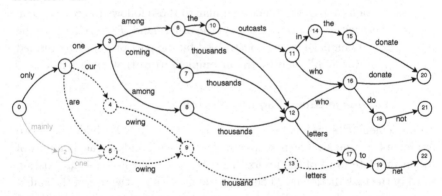

Fig. 4.8   Example of word-graph based interaction at the character level after the user has validated the prefix "only on". The edges (1, 4) and (1, 5) whose associated words do not begin with "on", are disabled.

4.7   Experimental Framework

The experimental framework adopted to assess the effectiveness of the CATTI system presented in this chapter is described in the following subsections. It includes experiments to test both the whole-word and the character interaction levels and also experiments to test the interaction with pointer actions.

The experiments have been performed using the three off-line corpora presented in Chap. 2 with the same assumptions made in Sec. 3.2.4.

4.7.1 *Assessment Measures*

Different objective evaluation measures, based on labelled test corpora, have been used in the experiments.

As discussed in Chap. 3, the quality of non-interactive transcription can be properly assessed with the well known Word Error Rate (WER) and Character Error Rate (CER) measures. The WER is also a reasonably good estimate of the human effort needed to *post-edit* the output of a *non-interactive* HTR recognizer at the word level. In contrast, the CER can not be considered a fair post-editing effort estimate at the character level because ignores the possibility of using an "advanced" word processor which may provide word "auto–completing" capabilities . Therefore we make an alternative definition of CER which better (less pessimistically) estimates the effort needed to post-edit an HTR transcription with the help of word "auto–completing". The new measure is called "Post-editing Key Stroke Ratio" (PKSR). WER and PKSR are used as baselines for the interactive HTR approaches discussed in previous sections of this Chapter.

To estimate the human effort needed to interactively produce correct transcriptions using a CATTI system, complementary assessment measures are introduced here; namely, the Word Stroke Ratio (WSR), the Pointer Action Rate (PAR) and the Key Stroke Ratio (KSR). WSR and PAR are aimed at interactive word-level assessment, while KSR aims at evaluating character-level interactive performance. All these measures are defined as follow:

- WER (*Word Error Rate*) : Minimum number of (whole) words that need to be substituted, deleted or inserted to convert a sentence recognized by the HTR system into the reference transcriptions, divided by the total number of words in these transcriptions. The WER is computed from the Levenshtein distance explained in section 3.2.4.
- CER (*Character Error Rate*) : Defined as the WER but considering characters instead of words.
- WSR (*Word Stroke Ratio*) : Number of required interactive word corrections divided by the total number of reference words. After each

system hypothesis, the longest common prefix between the hypothesis and the reference is obtained and the first mismatching word from the hypothesis is replaced ("corrected") with the corresponding reference word. This process is iterated until a full match with the reference is achieved.

- KSR (*Key Stroke Ratio*) : Number of required interactive character corrections divided by the total number of reference characters. It is computed as the WSR but considering characters instead of words.

- PAR (*Pointer Action Rate*) : Number of additional pointer actions needed using the pointer action interaction mode, divided by the total number of reference words.

- PKSR (*Post-editing Key Stroke Ratio*) : It is computed as the WER with two changes: a) the cost of each word editing operation is defined in terms of the number of character-level operations involved, and b) the total cost is divided by the total number of characters in the reference transcriptions. The cost of a *substitution* within a word is computed as the KSR, but just for one word, rather than for a line or sentence. That is, the longest common prefix between the hypothesis and the reference words is obtained and the first mismatching character from the hypothesis is replaced with the correct one. The system proposes a different word beginning with the validated word prefix. If it is not the correct one, the process is iterated. Similarly, the *insertion* cost is computed as the number of characters (of the reference word) which need to be inserted. The first character of the reference word is introduced and the system completes it with a full task vocabulary word. If it is not the reference word, it is substituted with the correct one as previously explained. Finally, the *deletion* cost is one; it is equivalent to substitute the first character of the extra word with the blank space.

The definitions of WSR and WER make these measures directly comparable. Moreover, the relative difference between them gives us a good estimate of the reduction in human effort that can be achieved by using CATTI with respect to using a conventional HTR system followed by human post-editing. This *Estimated Effort Reduction* will be denoted as "EFR".

However, as discussed above, the comparison between CER and KSR can not be considered totally fair, because KSR is computed for CL-CATTI, which implicitly entails auto-completing, but CER assumes just a plain post-edition. Therefore we use the Post-editing Key Stroke Ratio (PKSR), which does allow direct and fair comparison with KSR. In this case we assume that, when the user enters a character to correct some incorrect word, the "advanced" word processor would automatically complete the word with the most probable word in the task vocabulary. Obviously, the rest of the sentence would not change.

As with the WER and the WSR at the word level, the relative difference between PKSR and KSR gives us a good estimate of the reduction in human effort (EFR) that can be achieved by using CL-CATTI with respect to using a conventional HTR system followed by human post-editing with autocompleting. Note that EFR can also be used to compare CER with PKSR. In this case the the EFR estimates the post-editing effort saved by using an "advanced" word processor, with respect to a plain text editor.

Finally, to assess the pointer-based interaction mode of PA-CATTI, we use the PAR (*Pointer Action Rate*). Note that the additional human effort needed for the verification of the transcription and for positioning the cursor in the appropriate place in the conventional CATTI, is exactly the same as in (the first positioning action of) PA-CATTI. In both cases the user should read the transcription proposed by the system until finding an error and then he or she has to position the cursor at the place where the new word has to be typed.

4.7.2 *Parameters and Meta-Parameters*

Since CATTI is based on HMMs and N-grams, the meta-parameters corresponding to the design of these models need to be adjusted. As previously mentioned, the number of meta-parameters under discussion is totally negligible as compared with the overall number of model parameters (millions of N-gram, Gaussian, and state-transition parameters) which, are trained using only the training partitions. In experiments discussed below, the best models obtained for each task in the previous chapter for conventional HTR are directly used. It is important to note that CATTI does not need more parameters than those needed by the conventional HTR system.

We acknowledge that the meta-parameters for plain HTR where optimized in Chap. 3 for best test data accuracy and therefore, the absolute values of the results presented in the next section can be considered optimistic. On the other hand, we should take into account that interactive operation has not been assumed for model training or meta-parameter optimization. So, in this sense, absolute values of the results can be considered pessimistic with respect to the results which could be achieved by taking advantage of the interactive framework to train the models and optimize the meta-parameters. In any case, we should point out that relative differences, such as EFR, do provide us with valuable information about the advantages of interactive systems with respect to batch post-editing, which is in fact the important issue here.

On other hand, as explained on Sec. 4.4.2, when word-graph search is adopted in CATTI, an additional meta-parameter is needed: γ (Error Correcting Penalty – ECP) which weights the error-correcting cost with respect to the other model scores. To tune the ECP the following values were tested of this meta-parameter: 100, 200, 300, 400, 500 and 600.

4.8   Results

Here the results obtained with the different approaches proposed in this chapter are shown. First, we performed experiments using the Viterbi-based approach to make sure that the CATTI system presented here could be useful for the user and save human effort. Then, experiments were carried out using the word-graph based approach which, although it can loose some accuracy, incurres a much lower computational cost, actually allowing the user to interact with the system in real time. Then, results using PA in the CATTI interaction process are reported. Finally, some experiments at the character-level, that can allow for more ergonomic and friendly interfaces, are carried out.

Direct Viterbi-based approach

In the experiments carried out here, we have used the same meta-parameters values employed to obtain the baseline, non-interactive results presented in Sec. 3.2.6. Table 4.1 shows the estimated interactive human effort (WSR) required for each task, in comparison with the corresponding estimated post-editing effort (WER from Table 3.12). It also shows the estimated effort reduction (EFR), computed as the relative difference between WER and WSR.

According to these results, to produce 100 words of a correct transcription in the ODEC task, for example, a CATTI user should have to type only less than 20 words; the remaining 80 are automatically predicted by CATTI. That is to say, the CATTI user would save about 80% of the (typing and, in part thinking) effort needed to produce all the text manually. On the other hand, when interactive transcription is compared with post-editing,

Table 4.1 Performance of non-interactive off-line HTR (WER) and CATTI (WSR), along with the relative difference between them (Estimated Effort-Reduction – EFR) using the Viterbi-based search. All results are percentages.

Corpus	WER	WSR	EFR
ODEC	22.9	18.9	17.5
IAMDB	25.3	21.1	16.6
CS-page	28.5	26.9	5.7
CS-book	33.5	32.1	4.2

from every 100 (non-interactive) word errors, the CATTI user should have to interactively correct only less than 83. The remaining 17 errors would be automatically corrected by CATTI, thanks to the feedback information derived from other interactive corrections. It is important to remember here that these results do not take into account the errors due to page segmentation into lines. This fact may affect optimistically to the comparation between producing all the text manually and use the CATTI system. However, it does not affect the comparison between the post-editing approach and the CATTI system, because, in both cases, it is necessary to previously correct the errors of page segmentation into lines.

The different performance figures achieved in the different tasks can be explained by quality differences in the original images and also by the relative lexicon sizes and bi-gram estimation robustness (see Chap. 2). The later is particularly problematic in the case of CS which, in addition, suffers from a segmentation into relatively short, syntactically meaningless lines, which further hinders the ability of the bi-gram language model to capture relevant contextual information.

On the other hand, it is interesting to realize that CATTI is more effective for lines or sentences that have several errors; clearly, if a sentence has just one (word) error, it *must* be interactively corrected by the user and the best CATTI can do is to keep the remaining text unchanged. Obviously, this is not guaranteed by Eq. (4.1) and, in the worst case, a single word change made by the user may lead to more errors; that is, WSR $\geq$ WER. To analyse this behaviour, Fig. 4.9 presents WER, WSR and EFR values for increasing initial numbers of errors per sentence.

As expected, the estimated effort reduction increases with the number of errors per sentence, which clearly assess the ability of CATTI to correct more than one error per interaction step in sentences with several misrecognized words. Also, for sentences with a single error, CATTI does not help

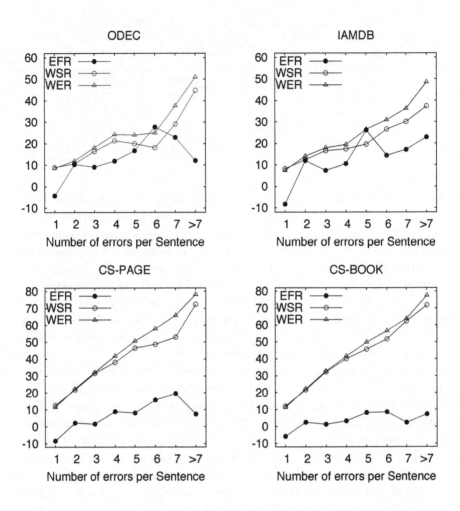

Fig. 4.9   WER, WSR and EFR (all in %) for varying number of errors per sentence.

at all or is even slightly worse than post-editing. Therefore, in practice, a good implementation of a CATTI user interface should allow the user to disable CATTI predictions when doing some (single-word) corrections.

Taking this into account, Table 4.2 shows the same results of Table 4.1, but excluding from the computation all the sentences with zero and one errors. As expected, the estimated effort reductions are better under this assumption.

Table 4.2 Performance of non-interactive off-line HTR (WER) and CATTI (WSR), along with the relative difference between them (Estimated Effort-Reduction – EFR), excluding the sentences with zero and one post-editing errors. All reported results are percentages.

Corpus	WER	WSR	EFR
ODEC	30.7	25.2	17.9
IAMDB	30.2	24.6	18.4
CS-page	36.7	34.1	6.9
CS-book	42.0	40.0	4.8

Word-graph based approach

In Fig. 4.10 we can see the WSR and the EFR obtained for each task using word-graphs search for different values of the error-correcting penalty γ in comparison with the corresponding WER. The word-graphs used in the experiments were generated with the same meta-parameters values used for the baseline results and the word-graph density is around 300. Table 4.3 summarizes the best WSR and EFR obtained for each task.

Table 4.3 Performance of non-interactive off-line HTR (WER) and CATTI (WSR), along with the relative difference between them (Estimated Effort-Reduction – EFR) using the word-graph based search. All results are percentages.

Corpus	WER	WSR	EFR
ODEC	22.9	21.5	6.1
IAMDB	25.3	22.5	11.1
CS-page	28.5	27.7	2.8
CS-book	33.5	32.3	3.6

According to these results and just as we expected, the results obtained using the direct Viterbi based search are better than those obtained with word-graphs. This is owing to the fact that the word-graph is just a pruned version of the Viterbi search trellis. Therefore, not all the possible transcriptions for the input handwritten text image are available, leading to some loose in system prediction accuracy. However, the computational cost of using word-graphs is much lower than using the direct Viterbi adaptation, actually allowing real time interaction. Note that, the higher the density of the WG, the better the accuracy. However, the size of the word graph grows with density, therefore we must find a compromise between size and accuracy.

As previously explained, CATTI is more effective for lines or sentences

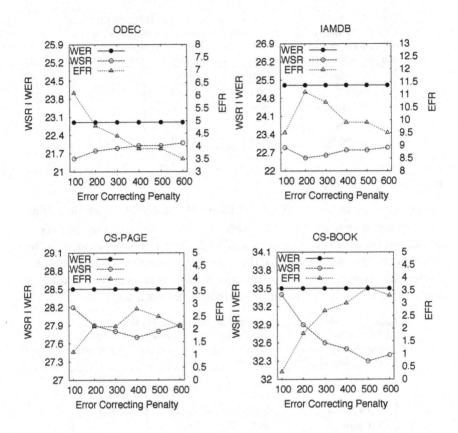

Fig. 4.10   WER, WSR and EFR (all in %) for different values of the parameter γ.

that have several errors. Figure 4.11 presents for word-graphs search the same results as those in Fig. 4.9. Also using WG search, the EFR increases with the number of errors per sentence. Table 4.4 shows the same results of Table 4.2, but using word graphs. As it happened using direct Viterbi search, the EFR is better if we only take into account the sentences with more than one error.

Using Pointer Actions in the CATTI interaction process (PA-CATTI)

As commented before, in order to be effective and fully useful, the PA-CATTI approach requires very short response times to emit a new suffix each time a pointer-action (PA) is performed. Therefore a search imple-

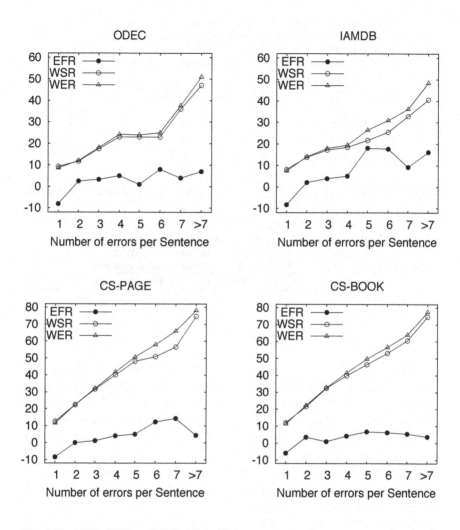

Fig. 4.11   WER, WSR and EFR (all in %) for varying number of errors per sentence.

mentation based on WG techniques is the only solution which fits this requirement. Table 4.5 shows the results obtained with the SPA interaction mode, which does not involve any extra human effort (see Sec. 4.5). The fist row shows the WSR obtained using SPA interaction (SPA-WSR). In the second row we can see the relative difference between the SPA-WSR with respect to the WSR obtained using the conventional CATTI (Table 4.3). Finally, the last row shows the estimated effort reduction using SPA inter-

Table 4.4 Performance of non-interactive off-line HTR (WER) and CATTI (WSR), along with the relative difference between them (Estimated Effort-Reduction – EFR), excluding the sentences with zero and one post-editing errors using word graphs. All reported results are percentages.

Corpus	WER	WSR	EFR
ODEC	30.7	28.6	6.8
IAMDB	30.2	26.3	12.9
CS-page	36.7	35.3	3.8
CS-book	42.0	40.3	4.1

action with respect to using a conventional HTR system followed by human post-editing (WER of Table 4.3).

Table 4.5 Performance of the SPA CATTI interaction (SPA-WSR), and Estimated Effort-Reduction of SPA-WSR with respect to WSR (EFR1) and SPA-WSR with respect to WER (EFR2). All results are percentages.

	ODEC	IAMDB	CS-PAGE	CS-BOOK
SPA-WSR	18.2	18.6	23.7	28.4
EFR1 (vsWSR)	15.3	17,3	14.4	12.1
EFR2 (vsWER)	20.5	26.5	16.8	15.2

According to Table 4.5, the estimated human effort to produce error-free transcriptions using PAs is significantly reduced with respect to using a conventional HTR system or the conventional CATTI (in both direct Viterbi and WG approximations). For example, in the IAMDB task, the new interaction mode can save about 26% of the overall effort, whereas the conventional CATTI would only save 11.1% using the word-graph approach, or 16.6% using the Viterbi search. It is important to remember here that, the Pointer-Action that the user makes in the SPA scenario do not involve any extra human effort.

Figure 4.12 shows the WSR, the Estimated Effort-Reduction (EFR) with respect to WER and the Pointer Action Rate (PAR) as a function of the maximal number of PAs allowed by the user before writing the correct word. The first point (0) corresponds to the results of the conventional CATTI, and the point "S" corresponds to the SPA interaction considered in the previous table. A good trade-off is obtained when the maximum number of PAs is around 3, because a significant amount of expected human effort is saved with a fairly low number of extra clicks per word. Table 4.6 shows a summary of the results obtained when the number of explicit PAs allowed by the user is 3.

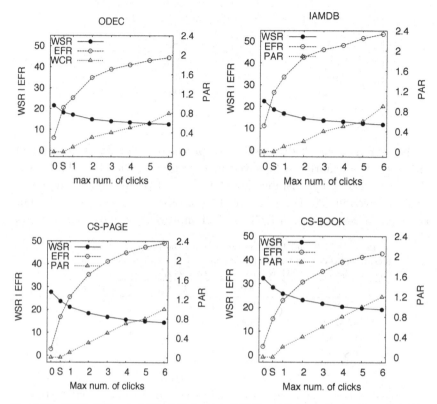

Fig. 4.12   WSR, Estimated Effort-Reduction (EFR) and Pointer Action Rate (PAR) as a function of the maximal number of explicit PA allowed by the user before writing the correct word. The first point (0) correspond to the conventional CATTI, and the point S correspond to the SPA interaction mode discussed in Sec. 4.5.

It is important to note that, the accuracy lost using WGs, instead of the direct Viterbi based approach, is more than recovered using PA-CATTI, leading to very significant expected effort reductions in all the cases. This interaction level can only be implemented using WGs due to its response time requirements.

CATTI at the character level

Table 4.7 shows the results obtained at the character level for the three corpora, CS on its page and book partitions, ODEC and IAMDB, using the plain HTR system without any system-user interactivity. Results confirm that only using a dictionary to autocomplete the words being corrected

Table 4.6   WSR, EFR and PAR for the different corpora when the number of explicit PAs allowed by the user before writing the correct word is 3.

Corpus	WSR	EFR	PAR
ODEC	14.0	38.9	0.4
IAMDB	13.6	46.2	0.4
CS-page	16.8	41.1	0.5
CS-book	21.7	35.2	0.6

by the user (i.e., and "advanced" word processor), significant amounts of human (typing) effort can be saved with respect to the plain HTR post-editing approach. For instance about to 15% of the human typing effort could be saved in CS. The PKSR results in table 4.7 are considered a fair baseline with respect to which CL-CATTI improvements have to be gauged.

Table 4.7   CER and PKSR obtained with the post-editing autocompleting approach on the HTR system. EFR for PKSR with respect to CER is also shown. All results are percentages.

CORPUS	CER	PKSR	EFR
ODEC	12.8	9.0	29.7
IAMDB	14.8	13.5	8.8
CS-page	15.4	12.9	16.2
CS-book	18.2	15.5	14.8

Table 4.8 shows the results obtained using CL-CATTI. As suggested by the KSR results, a CL-CATTI user could save as much as 87% or more typing effort with respect to a purely manual transcription process. On the other hand, in the column called "KSRvsCER" we can see the relative difference between using a CL-CATTI system with respect to using the plain HTR followed by raw post-editing. As discussed in the previous section, this comparison is not very fair, because KSR is computed for CL-CATTI, which implicitly entails autocompleting, but CER assumes just a raw post-editor[3]. On the other hand, the column called "KSRvsPKSR" shows a more fair comparison, where both compared results are computed assuming autocompleting. According to the results, the estimated human effort to produce error-free transcription using CL-CATTI is significantly reduced with respect to using the conventional HTR system with autocompleting

---

[3]This kind of comparison has been used in previous works in order to estimate the human effort that can be saved using interactive predictive processing with respect to post-editing [Tomás and Casacuberta (2006); Civera *et al.* (2004b)]. Therefore, we give here these figures for comparing purpose.

post-editing. More specifically, CL-CATTI saves around 16% of the overall estimated effort in the ODEC dataset, around 19% in the CS and close to 30% in IAMDB. overall effort.

Table 4.8 KSR obtained with the CATTI autocompleting approach. EFR for KSR with respect to CER and KSR with respect to PKSR are also shown. All results are percentages.

CORPUS	KSR	EFR	
		KSRvsCER	KSRvsPKSR
ODEC	7.5	41.4	16.6
IAMDB	9.6	35.1	28.9
CS-page	10.5	31.8	18.6
CS-book	12.5	30.7	18.7

4.9 Conclusions and Future Work

In this chapter, we have proposed a new interactive, on-line framework, which combines the efficiency of automatic HTR systems with the accuracy of the expert transcribers in the transcription of handwritten documents. In this proposal, the words corrected by the expert become part of a increasingly longer prefixes of the final target transcription. These prefixes are used by the CATTI system to suggest new suffixes that the expert can interactively accept or modify until a satisfactory, correct target transcription is finally produced.

This system has been tested in three different tasks, ODEC, IAMDB and CS. These tasks involve the transcription of handwritten answers from survey forms, handwritten full English sentences of different categories and an ancient handwritten document written in the XIX century, respectively. Given the extreme difficulty that entails the corpora used in the experiments, the obtained results are encouraging and show that the CATTI approach can significantly speed up the human transcription process.

Two different implementations have been tested. The first one is directly based on the Viterbi algorithm, whereas the other one is based on word-graph techniques. From the obtained results we can conclude, that, although the results obtained using the direct Viterbi-based approach are better, the word-graph approach is preferable. It is because the accuracy lost using word-graphs is not too high, while, the computational cost is much lower. This allows the human transcriber to actually interact with the system in real time.

In order to make the CATTI interaction process more comfortable, we have proposed another way to interact with the CATTI system, by considering PAs as an additional information source: as soon as the user points to the next system error, the system proposes a new, hopefully more correct continuation. We have shown that this user feedback can produce significant word stroke reductions, without any increase in interaction overhead. A simple implementation using word-graphs has been described and some experiments have been carried out. It is worth noting that alternative (n-best) suffixes could also be obtained with the conventional CATTI system. However, by considering the rejected words to propose the alternative suffixes, the PA-CATTI interaction methods here studied seem more effective and more comfortable for the user.

In this chapter, character level interaction has been studied too. The interaction in conventional CATTI was in the form of whole-word interactions. In the character interaction level, as soon as the user introduces a new character the system proposes a new suitable suffix. A simple implementation of this interaction level using word-graphs has been described and the corresponding experiments have been carried out. Considering the results obtained in the experiments, we can conclude that using this new interaction level not only allows for a more ergonomic and friendly interfaces, but significant amounts of human effort in the handwritten text transcription process can be saved. For example, in the page partition of the CS corpus, 18.6% of human effort can be saved, whereas using the CATTI system at word-level interaction, the estimated human effort reduction was around 2.8%.

It is worth noting, however, that results obtained at the character and word levels are not directly comparable. A word-level correction encapsulates fairly well all the cognitive and physical human efforts needed to locate an error and type the correction. This is true both for off-line editing (WER) and for CATTI corrections (WSR) and therefore word-level EFR figures can be considered quite fair. However, it is also clear that word-level corrections are less comfortable to users, in general. On the other hand, character-level corrections are much preferred by users, but it is unclear whether the number of keystrokes can be fairly used for assessment purposes. A corrective keystroke generally needs no significant cognitive effort since, in most cases, it is part of the correction of an already detected error. In other words, nor the CER (or the PKSR) neither the KSR account well for the cognitive component of corrective actions and it does not seem easy to establish a single, adequate scalar score that captures correctly the two kinds of human efforts involved at the character level. In the future we plan to carry out field tests which will hopefully provide a more realistic assessment of the relative advantages of interacting at the character or at the word level.

Given that the accuracy that can be obtained using the WGs grows with the WG density. In future, an optimization of this density will be carried out, in order to obtain better compromises between WG size and accuracy.

Chapter 5

Multimodal Computer Assisted Transcription of Handwritten Text Images

5.1 Introduction

Furthering the goal of making the interaction process friendlier to the user, led us to the development of *Multimodal CATTI* (MM-CATTI) [Toselli *et al.* (2010, 2008)]. As discussed in Chap. 4, traditional peripherals like keyboard and mouse can be used to unambiguously provide the feedback associated with the validation and correction of the successive system predictions. Nevertheless, using more ergonomic multimodal interfaces should result in an easier and more comfortable human-machine interaction, at the expense of the feedback being less deterministic to the system. This is the idea underlying MM-CATTI, which focus on touchscreen communication, perhaps the most natural modality to provide the required feedback in CATTI systems. It is worth noting, however, that the use of this more ergonomic feedback modality necessarily comes at the cost of additional interaction steps needed to correct possible feedback decoding errors. Therefore, solving the multimodal interaction problem amounts to achieving a modality synergy where both main and feedback data streams help each-other to optimize overall performance.

As shown in Fig. 1.1 (bottom) of the Chap. 1, the successive system's transcription hypotheses can be easily displayed on the touchscreen and user feedback corrections can be made through on-line pen-strokes and text which are exactly written over the text produced by the system.

In Fig. 5.1 we can see a schematic view of the MM-CATTI system presented in this chapter. The main part of the system is the same presented in the Fig. 4.1 for CATTI. However, since the user feedback is now provided in form of pen-strokes, an on-line HTR subsystem is introduced. This HTR subsystem follows the same architecture as the main HTR system and it

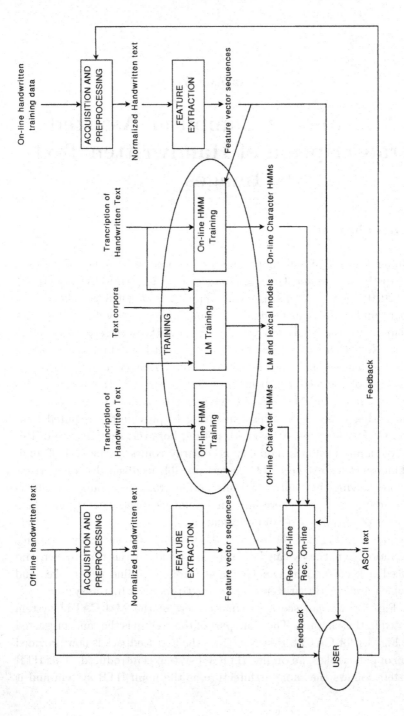

Fig. 5.1   Overview of the MM-CATTI system.

is in charge of decoding the feedback provided by the user. The feedback recognition module used here is adapted to take advantage of interaction-derived information to boost its on-line HTR accuracy.

5.2   Formal Framework

Let $\mathbf{x}$ be the input image and $\mathbf{s}$' the suffix suggested by the system as continuation of a prefix $\mathbf{p}$ consolidated in the previous interaction step. Hence, $\mathbf{ps}$' constitutes a whole recognized hypothesis. The user validates the longest prefix, $\mathbf{p}$', of the recognized hypothesis, $\mathbf{ps}$', which is error-free. Then he or she introduces some on-line *touchscreen pen strokes*[1], $\mathbf{t}$, to correct the erroneous text, v, that follows the validated prefix. Actually, the validated prefix $\mathbf{p}$' is implicitly (and deterministically) stated as a positioning information included as part of $\mathbf{t}$. Moreover, the user may additionally type some keystrokes (κ) on the keyboard in order to correct (other) parts of this suffix and/or to add more text. Using this information, the system has to suggest a new suffix, $\mathbf{s}$, for the next interaction, as a continuation of the user validated prefix $\mathbf{p}$', and using the on-line touchscreen strokes $\mathbf{t}$ and the typed text κ. That is, the problem is to find $\mathbf{s}$ given $\mathbf{x}$ and a feedback information composed of $\mathbf{p}', v, \mathbf{t}$ and κ, considering all possible *decodings*, d, of the on-line data $\mathbf{t}$ (i.e., letting d be a hidden variable):

$$\hat{\mathbf{s}} = \operatorname*{argmax}_{\mathbf{s}} \Pr(\mathbf{s} \mid \mathbf{x}, \mathbf{p}', \mathbf{t}, v, \kappa) = \operatorname*{argmax}_{\mathbf{s}} \sum_{d} \Pr(\mathbf{s}, d \mid \mathbf{x}, \mathbf{p}', \mathbf{t}, v, \kappa) \quad (5.1)$$

This general scenario can be seen as an instantiation of the problem already formulated in Eq. 1.8, where $(\mathbf{p}', v)$ and $(\mathbf{t}, \kappa)$ correspond to h' and f respectively. Therefore, assumptions and developments similar to those of Eqs 1.9-1.10 lead to:

$$\hat{\mathbf{s}} \approx \operatorname*{argmax}_{\mathbf{s}} \max_{d} P(\mathbf{x} \mid \mathbf{p}', v, d, \kappa, \mathbf{s}) \cdot P(\mathbf{s} \mid \mathbf{p}', v, d, \kappa)$$
$$\cdot P(d \mid \mathbf{p}', v) \cdot P(\mathbf{t} \mid d) \quad (5.2)$$

Eq. 5.2 generally involves several difficulties and it seldom admits exact and efficient search solutions. A simple approximation which consists in decomposing Eq. 5.2 into a two-phase computation is presented here.

According to the above very general discussion, it might be assumed that the user can type with independence of the result of the on-line handwritten

---

[1] *Pen strokes* are assumed to be sequences of real-valued vectors. See Sec. 3.3 for details.

decoding process. However, it can be argued that this generality is not realistically useful in practical situations. Alternatively, it is much more natural that the user waits for a specific system outcome ($\hat{d}$) from the on-line touchscreen interaction data ($\mathbf{t}$), prior to start typing amendments (κ) to the (remaining part of the previous) system hypothesis. Furthermore, this allows the user to fix possible on-line handwritten recognition errors in $\hat{d}$.

In the first phase of this more pragmatic and simpler scenario, the user produces some on-line touchscreen data $\mathbf{t}$ (to correct the erroneous text v) and the system has to decode $\mathbf{t}$ into some text $\hat{d}$ using the validated prefix $\mathbf{p}'$, but ignoring information directly related with the main data $\mathbf{x}$:

$$\hat{d} \approx \underset{d}{\operatorname{argmax}} P(d \mid \mathbf{p}', v) \cdot P(\mathbf{t} \mid d) \qquad (5.3)$$

This corresponds to approximately solving Eq. 5.2 for d, ignoring the first two terms. Once $\hat{d}$ is available, Eq. 5.2 can be approximately solved using $d = \hat{d}$ and ignoring the last two terms. To this end, the user enters the amendment keystrokes κ, if necessary, and produce a new consolidated prefix $\mathbf{p}$, based on the previous $\mathbf{p}'$, v, $\hat{d}$ and κ. This leads to the following expression, identical to Eq. 4.1:

$$\hat{\mathbf{s}} \approx \underset{\mathbf{s}}{\operatorname{argmax}} P(\mathbf{x} \mid \mathbf{p}, \mathbf{s}) \cdot P(\mathbf{s} \mid \mathbf{p}) \qquad (5.4)$$

The process continues in this way until $\mathbf{p}$ is accepted by the user as a full correct transcription of $\mathbf{x}$.

An example of this kind of inter-leaved off-line image recognition and on-line touchscreen interaction is shown in Fig. 5.2. In this example, we are assuming that on-line handwriting is the modality preferred by the user to make corrections, relaying on the keyboard mainly (or only) to correct eventual on-line text decoding errors. Note that the potential increase in comfort of this setting comes at expense of a hopefully small number of additional interaction steps using the keyboard. In this example the user would need *three* interactive corrections using MM-CATTI, compared with the two keyboard-only corrections using CATTI and with the *six* post-editing word corrections required by the original, non interactively recognized hypothesis.

Since we have already dealt with Eq. (5.4) in Chap. 4 (Eq. (4.1)-(4.4)), we focus now on Eq. (5.3). As in Chap. 3, $P(\mathbf{t} \mid d)$ is provided by (HMM) morphological models of the text in d (see Sec. 3.3.3 for details). On the other hand, here, $P(d \mid \mathbf{p}', v)$ can be provided by a language model constrained by information derived from the previous prefix $\mathbf{p}'$ and by the

	x	*only one among thousands who do not.*						
INTER-0	p							
	ŝ ≡ ŵ	only	our	owing	thousand	letters	to	net
	p', t	only	*one*					
INTER-1	d̂		onu					
	κ		e					
	p	only	one					
	ŝ			among	thousands	letters	to	net
	p', t	only	one	among	thousands	**who**		
INTER-2	d̂					who		
	κ							
	p	only	one	among	thousands	who		
	ŝ						do	not
FINAL	κ							#
	p ≡ T	only	o<u>n</u>e	among	thousands	*who*	do	not

Fig. 5.2   Example of multimodal CATTI interaction with a CATTI system, to transcribe an image of the handwritten sentence *"only one among thousands who do not"*. Each interaction step starts with a transcription prefix **p** that has been fixed in the previous step. First, the system suggests a suffix **ŝ** and the user handwrites some touchscreen text, **t**, to amend **ŝ**. This defines a correct prefix **p'**, which can be used by the on-line HTR subsystem to obtain a decoding of **t**. After observing this decoding, $\hat{d}$, the user may type additional keystrokes, κ, to correct possible errors in $\hat{d}$ (and perhaps to amend other parts of **ŝ**). A new prefix, **p**, is built from the previous correct prefix **p'**, the decoded on-line handwritten text, $\hat{d}$, and the typed text κ. The process ends when the user enters the special character "**#**". System suggestions are printed in boldface and typed text in typewriter font. In the final transcription, **T**, handwritten text is in italic fonts and typed text is additionally underlined. Assuming all interactions as whole-word corrections, the post editing WER would be 6/7 (85%), while the MM-CATTI WSR is 3/7 (43%); i.e., 2 touch-screen plus 1 keyboard word corrections.

erroneous text that follows it, v. Equation (5.3) may lead to several scenarios depending on the assumptions and constraints adopted for $P(d \mid \mathbf{p'}, v)$. We examine some of them hereafter.

The simplest one corresponds to a conventional, non-interactive on-line HTR setting, where all the available conditions are ignored; i.e., $P(d \mid \mathbf{p'}, v) \equiv P(d)$. This is considered here as a *baseline*.

A more informative setting arises by taking into account the erroneous text, v. The user introduces the touchscreen data, **t**, in order to correct the wrong text, v, that follows the validated prefix **p'**. Therefore, we can assume an *error-conditioned* model such as $P(d \mid \mathbf{p'}, v) \equiv P(d \mid v)$; clearly, knowing the word that the user has already deemed incorrect should prevent the on-line decoder making the same error.

If, in addition to v, the information derived from the accepted prefix is also taken into account, a particularly useful scenario arises. In this case the decoding of **t** is further constrained to be a suitable continuation of the prefix accepted so far, **p'**; that is, the full $P(d \mid \mathbf{p'}, v)$ is used. This multimodal model, referred to as MM-CATTI [Toselli *et al.* (2008)], is the one studied in detail in this chapter.

5.3 Adapting the Language Model

Language modelling and search techniques needed for the on-line HTR feedback subsystem in MM-CATTI are essentially similar to those described in Sec. 4.3 for the main, off-line HTR system. Language model constraints are implemented on the base of n-grams, depending on each multimodal scenario considered.

The simplest *baseline* scenario does not take into account any interaction-derived information and $P(d)$ could be provided by the same n-gram used for the off-line decoder. To simplify matters (and to better approach predictive usage patterns of MM-CATTI), only single-word touch-screen corrections are considered. That is, v is assumed to be the text of a single whole word and, therefore, only uni-grams actually make sense for $P(d)$.

The single-word assumption also simplifies the *error-conditioned* language model, $P(d \mid v)$, as follows:

$$P(d \mid v) = \begin{cases} 0 & d = v \\ \dfrac{P(d)}{1 - P(v)} & d \neq v \end{cases} \tag{5.5}$$

Finally, in the complete MM-CATTI the feedback language model is $P(d \mid \mathbf{p'}, v)$. That is, the on-line HTR subsystem should produce a hypothesis $\hat{d}$ for the touchscreen strokes **t**, taking into account a user-accepted prefix, **p'**, and the first wrong word, v, in the off-line HTR suggestion. In this case, arguments similar to those in Sec. 4.5 apply and, under the single whole-word assumption, we can use Eq. 4.21 changing **s** with d, leading to:

$$P(d \mid \mathbf{p'}, v) = \begin{cases} 0 & d = v \\ \dfrac{P(d \mid \mathbf{p'}^{k}_{k-n+2})}{1 - P(v \mid \mathbf{p'}^{k}_{k-n+2})} & d \neq v \end{cases} \tag{5.6}$$

where k is the length of **p'**.

5.4   Searching

A simple implementation of Eq. 5.6 is illustrated in Fig. 5.3, corresponding to the same language model example of Fig. 4.3.   In this example, **p'** = "only one" and the user wants to correct the wrong off-line recognized word "thing", by handwriting the word "among" (for example) on the touchscreen. If the on-line HTR sub-system uses a bi-gram model, it is conditioned by the context word "one" (which is now the initial state) and the word transition edge "thing" is disabled.

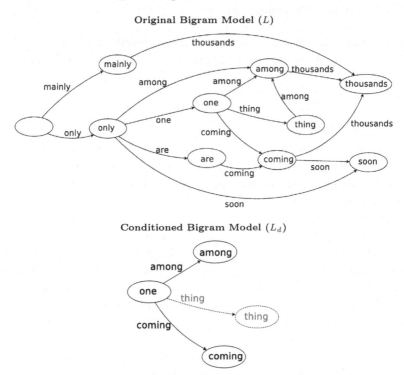

Fig. 5.3   Example of MM-CATTI dynamic bi-gram language model generation for on-line HTR feedback decoding. *L* is the original bi-gram model used by the off-line HTR system, whereas L_d is the bi-gram sub-model, derived from *L*, which takes as initial state that corresponding to the prefix "one". This simplified language model is used by the on-line HTR sub-system to recognize the touchscreen handwritten word "among", intended to replace the wrong off-line recognized word "thing", which was disabled in L_d.

As shown in the example, and unlike it happened in CATTI, the linear language model of the prefix **p'** is no longer required, because the corresponding on-line touchscreen data of the prefix **p'** do no exist in this case. Moreover, as we are assuming single whole-word corrections, only the direct transitions from the starting node (the "**one**" node in the example) need to be considered.

As in CATTI searching (Sec. 4.4), owing to the finite-state nature of the n-gram language model, the search involved in Eq. (5.6) can be efficiently carried out using the Viterbi algorithm.

5.5 Experimental Framework

The experimental framework adopted to assess the effectiveness of the MM-CATTI system presented in this chapter is described in the following subsections.

5.5.1 *Corpora*

The experiments have been performed using the three off-line corpora presented in Chap. 2, with the same assumptions made in Sec. 3.2.4. To train the on-line HTR feedback subsystem and test the MM-CATTI approach, the on-line handwriting UNIPEN corpus was chosen. As explained in Sec. 2.5, the UNIPEN data come organized into several categories such as lower and uppercase letters, digits symbols, isolated words and full sentences. Unfortunately, the isolated words category does not contain all (or almost none of) the required word instances that would have to be handwritten by the user in the MM-CATTI interaction process with the ODEC, IAMDB, or CS text images. Therefore, these words were generated by concatenating random character instances from three UNIPEN categories: $1a$ (digits), $1c$ (lowercase letters) and $1d$ (symbols).

To increase realism, the generation of each of these test words was carried out employing characters belonging to the same writer. Three arbitrary writers were chosen, taking care that sufficient samples of all the characters needed for the generation of the required word instances were available from each writer. Each character needed to generate a given word was plainly aligned along a common word baseline, except if it had a descender, in which case the character baseline was raised 1/3 of its height. The horizontal separation between characters was randomly selected from *one* to *three* trajectory points. The selected writers are identified by their name initials as BS, BH and BR. Figure 5.4 shows examples of on-line word samples generated in this way, along with real samples of the same words written by two writers in our labs.

Words from concatenated UNIPEN chars	Real word writing
prendas prendas prendos	prendas prendas
while while while	while while

Fig. 5.4 Examples of words generated using characters from the three selected UNIPEN test writers (BH, BR, BS), along with samples of the same words written by two other writers in our labs. By comparison, generated samples are quite realistic.

Training data were produced in a similar way using 17 different UNIPEN writers. For each of these writers, one sample of each of the 42 symbols and digits needed was randomly selected and one sample of each of the 1 000 most frequent Spanish words and the 1 000 most frequent English words was generated, resulting in 34 714 training tokens (714 isolated characters plus 34 000 generated words). To generate these tokens, 186 881 UNIPEN character instances were used, using as many repetitions as required out of the 17 177 *unique* character samples available. Table 5.1 summarizes the amount of UNIPEN training and test data used in our experiments.

Table 5.1 Basic statistics of the UNIPEN training and test data used in the experiments.

Number of different:	Train	Test	Lexicon
writers	17	3	-
digits (1a)	1 301	234	10
letters (1c)	12 298	2 771	26
symbols (1d)	3 578	3 317	32
total characters	17 177	6 322	68

5.5.2 *Assessment Measures*

In order to assess the MM-CATTI system accuracy, different evaluation measures have been adopted. As in Chap. 4 the WER and the WSR are used to asses the quality of non-interactive transcriptions and the CATTI system respectively. The WSR of the MM-CATTI system will be decomposed into TS (touchscreen) and KBD (Keyboard). TS represents the percentage of corrections successfully made through the on-line HTR feedback modality. KBD is the percentage of corrections for which the feedback decoder failed and the correction would have to be entered by means of the keyboard. On the other hand, as in CATTI, the EFR will give us an estimate of the reduction in human effort that can be achieved by using MM-CATTI with respect to using a conventional HTR system followed by human post-editing.

Finally, since only single-word corrections are considered, the conventional classification error rate (ER) will be used to assess the accuracy of the on-line HTR feedback subsystem under the different constraints entailed by the MM-CATTI interaction process.

5.6   Results

The aim of these experiments is to assess the effectiveness of MM-CATTI in the scenarios described in Sec. 5.2. Multimodal operation offers ergonomy and increased usability at the expense of the system having to deal with non-deterministic feedback signals. Therefore, the main concern here is the accuracy of the on-line HTR feedback decoder and the experiments mainly aim to determine how much this accuracy can be boosted by taking into account information derived from the proper interaction process. Ultimately, experiments aim at assessing which degree of synergy can actually be expected by taking into account both interactivity and multimodality.

In order to establish a word decoding baseline accuracy for the on-line HTR feedback subsystem, a simple word recognition experiment was carried out. As discussed in Sec. 5.5.1, the words needed to train and test the feedback subsystem for each task were generated by concatenating adequate UNIPEN characters. Therefore, new character HMMs were trained from these training words, using the meta-parameters previously tuned through the isolated character recognition experiments discussed in Sec. 3.3.5. On the other hand, since only single words have to be recognized, a uni-gram language model was trained for each off-line task (CS-page, CS-book, ODEC and IAMDB) to estimate the corresponding word prior probabilities.

Table 5.2 shows the basic statistics of the data used in this experiment, along with the ER achieved by the non-interactive on-line HTR subsystem in the different tasks, using GSF values optimized for each language model. The words used as feedback correspond to the words that the user would have to introduce in a standard CATTI iteration process using an implementation based on the direct Viterbi search approach. That is, these words are these "word strokes" used to compute the WSR presented in table 4.1. Note that if a WG-search implementation had been used, slightly different words and/or number of their instances would have been obtained. Nevertheless, as we will see in Chap. 6, a demonstrator of MM-CATTI has been implemented using an hybrid search decoding scheme; that is, off-line HTR decoding is based on WGs, whereas feedback decoding relies directly on Viterbi.

Note that these ER values are obtained without taking advantage of any interaction-derived contextual information (i.e., just using plain unigrams). Therefore these figures represent the highest accuracies that could be expected if, e.g., an off-the-shelf on-line HTR system where adopted to implement the MM-CATTI feedback decoder.

Table 5.2 For each off-line HTR task: statistics of the sets of on-line words needed as feedback to correct the word errors made by the plain off-line HTR system. The right most column shows the baseline performance (classification error ER) of the corresponding on-line HTR subsystem without using any interaction-derived contextual information (i.e., using plain 1-grams).

Task	#Words	#Uniq-Words	Lexicon	ER(%)
ODEC	753	378	2 790	5.1
IAMDB	755	510	8 017	4.6
CS-page	1 196	648	2 277	6.4
CS-book	1 487	703	2 237	6.1

As explained in Sec. 5.2 information derived from the interaction process can be taken into account in order to improve the accuracy of the on-line HTR subsystem. Table 5.3 presents the writer average feedback decoding error rates for the ODEC, IAMDB, CS-page and CS-book corpora and three language models which embody increasingly strong interaction derived constraints. The first one is the plain unigram estimation of $P(d)$, already reported in Table 5.2 as a *baseline*. The second is an error-conditioned unigram estimation of $P(d \mid v)$ (Eq. (5.5)). The third model is a prefix-and-error conditioned bi-gram estimate of $P(d \mid \mathbf{p'}, v)$ (Eq. (5.6)). All these models are derived from the original language models employed for the main, off-line HTR system, as explained in Sec. 5.4. As observed in Table 5.3, feedback decoding accuracy increases significantly as more interaction-derived constraints are taken into account.

Individual recognition error rates of each of the three UNIPEN writers used in the experiments are plotted in Fig. 5.5 for the different language models and corpora. The accuracy for the three writers is very similar, being WrBS who obtained the best results.

Table 5.3   Writer average MM-CATTI feedback decoding error rates for the different corpora and three language models: plain unigram (U, *baseline*), error-conditioned unigram (U_e) and prefix-and-error conditioned bi-gram (B_e). The relative accuracy improvement for B_e with respect to U is shown in the last column.

Corpus	Feedback ER (%)			Rel. Improv. (%)
	U	U_e	B_e	B_e
ODEC	5.1	5.0	3.1	39.2
IAMDB	4.6	4.3	3.5	23.9
CS-page	6.4	6.2	5.8	9.3
CS-book	6.1	5.9	5.5	8.2

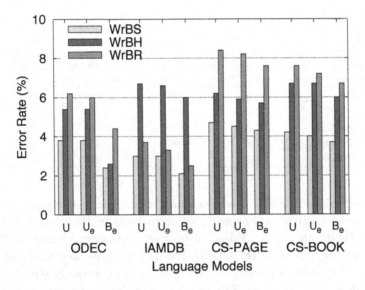

Fig. 5.5   MM-CATTI feedback decoding error rates for different writers, corpora and prefix-constrained language models.

Table 5.4 summarizes all the CATTI and MM-CATTI results obtained in this work. The third and forth columns show the CATTI WSR decomposed into the percentage of corrections successfully made through the on-line HTR feedback modality (the touch-screen, TS) and those for which the feedback decoder failed and the correction had to be entered by means of the keyboard (KBD). These figures correspond to the three-writers averaged decoding errors reported in Table 5.3. The last two columns show the overall estimated effort reductions (EFR) in the CATTI and MM-CATTI approaches. The MM-CATTI EFR is calculated under the simplifying

Table 5.4 From left-to-right: post-editing corrections (WER), interactive corrections needed (WSR), contributions of both input modalities: on-line touch-screen (TS) and keyboard (KBD), and overall estimated effort reduction (EFR) achieved by the proposed approaches. All results are percentages.

Corpus	Post-edit WER	CATTI WSR	MM-CATTI TS	MM-CATTI KBD	Overall EFR CATTI	Overall EFR MM-CATTI
ODEC	22.9	18.8	18.1	0.7	17.5	14.8
IAMDB	25.3	21.1	20,4	0,7	16.6	13.8
CS-page	28.5	26.9	25.4	1.5	5.6	0.4
CS-book	33.5	32.1	30,4	1,7	4.2	-0,8

(but reasonable) assumption that the cost of keyboard-correcting a feedback on-line decoding error is similar to that of another on-line touchscreen interaction step. That is, each KBD correction is counted twice: one for the failed touch-screen attempt and another for the keyboard correction itself.

According to these results, the expected user effort for the more ergonomic and user-preferred touch-screen based MM-CATTI, is only slightly higher than that of CATTI in the ODEC and on the IAMDB corpora. In the CS corpus the results shown that the expected user effort is very similar to the expected post-editing effort. However, with MM-CATTI, the effort is spent in an easier and friendlier human-machine interaction process.

5.7 Conclusions

In this chapter the use of on-line touch-screen handwritten pen strokes is studied as an alternative feedback modality for CATTI. We have called this approach "multimodal CATTI" (MM-CATTI). From the results, we observe that (in most cases) this more ergonomic feedback modality can be implemented without significantly increasing the number of interaction steps due to errors caused by the decoding of the feedback signals. This is achieved thanks to the constraints derived from the interactive process.

It should be mentioned here that, in addition to the laboratory experiments reported in previous section, a complete MM-CATTI prototype has been implemented (see Chap. 6) and already submitted to preliminary, informal tests with real users. According to these tests, the system does meet the expectations derived from the laboratory experiments; both in terms of usability and performance. This is particularly true for the on-line HTR feedback decoding accuracy: even though the on-line HTR

HMMs were trained from artificially built words using UNIPEN character samples, the accuracy in real operation with real users is observed to be similar to that shown in the laboratory results here reported. Of course even higher accuracy can be easily achieved by retraining the models with the text handwritten by the actual users.

Chapter 6

A Web-based Demonstrator of Interactive Multimodal Transcription

WITH CONTRIBUTION OF: Luis A. Leiva and Vicente Alabau

6.1 Introduction

In this chapter a web-based demonstrator of the interactive multimodal approach presented in this book is introduced. In this demonstrator the user feedback is provided by means of pen strokes on a touchscreen [Romero *et al.* (2009a,b)]. This user feedback allows to improve the system accuracy, while multimodality increases system ergonomics and user acceptability. Figure 1.1 (top) of the Chap. 1 shows a user interacting with this demo. Both the original image and the system's transcription hypotheses can be easily aligned and jointly displayed on the touchscreen (bottom).

Although, the present system is only a demonstrator, in a next future, we plan to evolve such web-based MM-CATTI system to allow users across the globe to carry out collaborative handwritten text transcription tasks. Since the users operate within a web browser window, the system also provides cross-platform compatibility and requires no disk space on the client machine.

A description of the user interaction protocol of the proposed demonstration is given in Sec. 6.2. Then, and overview of the demonstrator is detailed on Sec. 6.3. Later, some experiments carried out with real users are presented in Sec. 6.4-6.5. Finally, some results and conclusions are given in Sec. 6.6.

6.2   User Interaction Protocol

In the MM-CATTI web-based demonstrator, the user is directly involved in the transcription process. The protocol that rules this process was presented in the Chap. 5 and can be summarized in the following steps:

- The HTR system proposes a full transcription of an input handwritten text image.
- The user validates the longest prefix of the transcription which is error-free and enters some on-line touchscreen pen-strokes and/or some amendment keystrokes to correct the first error in the suffix.
- If pen strokes are available, an on-line HTR feedback subsystem is used to decode this input.
- In this way, a new extended consolidated prefix is produced based on the previous validated prefix, the on-line decoded word and the keystroke amendments. Using this new prefix, the MMCATTI system suggests a suitable continuation of it.
- These previous steps are iterated until a final, perfect transcription is produced.

The interaction between the user and the system is not only limited to writing fully correct words, but other different editing operations can be carried out using both pen-strokes and/or keystrokes. Note that each interactive editing operation generates a different prefix. The types of operations that can be carried out and the corresponding validated prefixes are:

- Substitution: The first erroneous word is replaced with the correct word. The validated prefix consists of all the words preceding the wrong word plus the new correct word.
- Deletion: An incorrect word between two correct words is deleted. The accepted prefix consists of all the words preceding the deleted word plus the word that follows the deleted word.
- Rejection: This operation corresponds with the Pointer Action operation studied in Sec. 4.5. All the words that precede the incorrect word constitute the validated prefix. The system proposes a new suffix where the first word is different to the incorrect word.
- Insertion: A new word is inserted between two correct words. The validated prefix is composed of all the word precedent the inserted word, the inserted word and the word that follows the inserted word.

• Accept Final Transcription: The proposed transcription is validated.

6.3   System Description

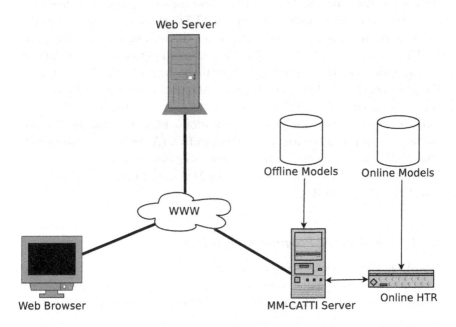

Fig. 6.1   Diagram of system architecture.

The demonstrator presented in this chapter is publicly available at "http://cat.iti.upv.es/iht". In this web-based demo the client-server communication is made through binary sockets [Alabau *et al.* (2009)]. Using sockets has several advantages over other communication channels. On the one hand it allows much faster message exchanging and lower latency responses. On the other hand, a multiuser environment can be easily implemented, so that, several users across the globe can work concurrently on the same task. In addition, the web server and the MM-CATTI server do not need to be physically at the same place. Therefore, a dedicated transcription server can be run per task to deal with high CPU demanding corpora, or several servers can be set up with the same task to serve an increasing amount of users.

Figure 6.1 shows a schematic view of the system's architecture. First, the web client requests a web page with an index of all available pages in the document to be transcribed. The user then navigates to a page and begins to transcribe the handwritten text images line by line. She can make corrections with pen strokes and also use the keyboard. If pen strokes are available, the MM-CATTI server uses an on-line HTR feedback subsystem (tightly coupled with MM-CATTI) to decode them. Finally, taking into account the decoded word an the off-line models, the MM-CATTI server responds with a suitable continuation to the prefix validated by the user. On the other hand, keystrokes data directly interact with the aforementioned MM-CATTI server. All corrections are stored in plain text logs on the MM-CATTI server, so the user can retake them in any moment. Other client-server communications, such as managing logs or loading the sockets interface, are made via AJAX (Asynchronous JavaScript And XML), providing thus a richer interactive experience.

On the next subsections the API, the MM-CATTI server and the Web Interface are described.

6.3.1 *Application Programming Interface*

Based on the previously presented protocol, a generic subset of primitives were identified, and a client-server Application Programming Interface (API) that allows client and server applications to communicate through sockets was designed.

Three basic functions summarize the API:

- **set_source** : selects the source phrase to be transcribed.
- **set_prefix** : sets the longest error free prefix and amends the first error with the keyboard.
- **set_prefix_online** : sets the longest error free prefix and amends the first error with pen strokes.

6.3.2 *MM-CATTI Server*

The MM-CATTI server combines all the information received from the client and computes a suitable prediction. It follows the approach presented on Chap. 5, where both on-line and off-line HTR systems are based on HMM and n-gram language models.

The off-line system is implemented using word-graphs. Each of these word-graphs is a pruned version of the Viterbi search trellis obtained when transcribing the whole image sentence. In order to make the system able to interact with the user in a time efficient way, they are computed beforehand.

Once the user selects the line to be transcribed, the client application sends to the MM-CATTI server a **set_source** message. The MM-CATTI server loads the word-graph corresponding to the selected line and proposes a full transcription as explained in Sec. 3.2.

When the user makes some correction, if pen strokes are available, the MM-CATTI server decodes them by means of the on-line HTR feedback subsystem. After preprocessing and extracting the features, as it is explained in Sec. 3.3, the pen strokes are decoded following the last scenario presented in Chap. 5, taking into account information derived from the validated prefix and the previous suffix as shown Eq. (5.6).

Once the pen strokes have been decoded, a new prefix is generated taking into account the validated prefix, the new decoded word and the operation that the user has carried out (substitution, deletion, insertion, etc). Then, this new prefix is parsed in the off-line word-graph and a suitable continuation is provided following techniques described in Chap. 4. It may happen that the prefix is not in the word-graph; so, the error correcting parsing explained in Sec. 4.4 is applied.

6.3.3   Web Interface

The Web Interface is responsible for showing the user interface and capturing the user actions of the different modalities of interaction, i.e, keyboard and pen strokes.

In the main page of the demonstrator, the user must choose one of the available documents to transcribe by clicking on the *"transcribe"* button. Also, by clicking on *"use custom server?"* link (see Fig. 6.3), the user can specify a custom MM-CATTI server for specific research purposes while her session is active. In addition, in this page a lot of information related with the demonstrator is provided, such as the usage instructions, videos, awards, news or publications. Fig. 6.2 shows a screen capture of this main page.

Once the user has selected the document to transcribe, a new web page with an index of all pages in the corpus appears, allowing the user navigate to any page. In Fig. 6.4 we can see the different pages of the nineteenth century legacy handwritten document CS.

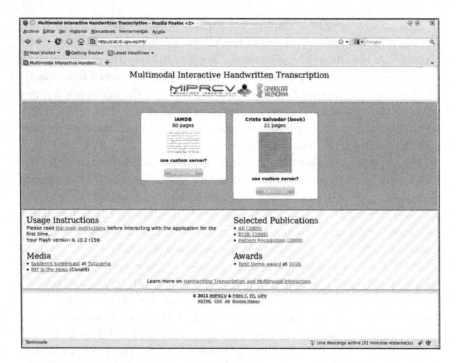

Fig. 6.2   The main page of the web-based demonstrator. In addition the documents to transcribe, a lot of information related with it is shown: usage instructions, videos, awards, news and publications.

To begin with, once the user selects a thumbnail page from the index, the full page is loaded (Fig. 6.5). The center block is the page to transcribe itself. The tidy menu on the right side is a pagination item to allow the user browsing all pages quickly. By using the page browser located below the center page, the user can browse all the pages visually. The bottom menu is intended to help the user with common tasks, such as closing session, changing the document to transcribe, displaying application shortcuts, or exploring the API.

Then, the user can select a line from the current page by clicking on it, and the system will propose an initial, full transcription (see Fig. 6.6). If no error is detected, the user chooses another text line to be transcribed. Otherwise, the user validates a prefix of the transcription which is error-free and corrects the first error in the suffix.

If an *e-pen* is available, as previously discussed, the system uses the on-line HTR feedback subsystem to recognize the user corrective pen-

Fig. 6.3 By clicking on *"use custom server?"* link, the user can specify a custom CATTI server while her session is active.

strokes. Then, taking into account the (multimodal) user corrections, the system responds with a suitable continuation to the prefix validated by the user.

The interaction between user and system can be carried out using pen-strokes on a touchscreen or using traditional peripherals like keyboard and mouse. In the next subsections these different interactions modes are explained.

6.3.4   *Electronic Pen or Touchscreen Interaction*

This is the default interaction modality. The application can be used with any kind of pointing device, such as an electronic pen or a PC tablet. The computer mouse can be also used. However, this option is discouraged because typical computer mice, are inadequate for writing with precision.

By using pen-strokes, the user can directly write the correct word, or also introduce some gestures to indicate different error types. These intuitive pen-based gestures greatly simplify the error correction effort. In Fig. 6.7 the available gestures are shown:

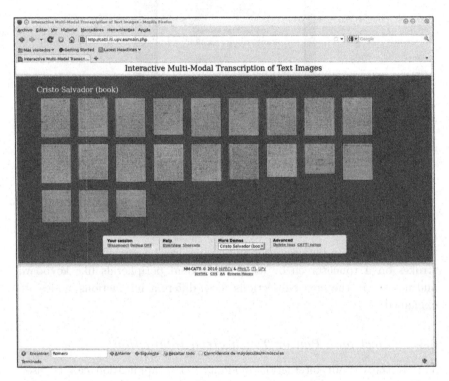

Fig. 6.4 A thumbnail for each page of the document chosen by the user is shown. In this case the thumbnails belong to pages of the "Cristo Salvador" book.

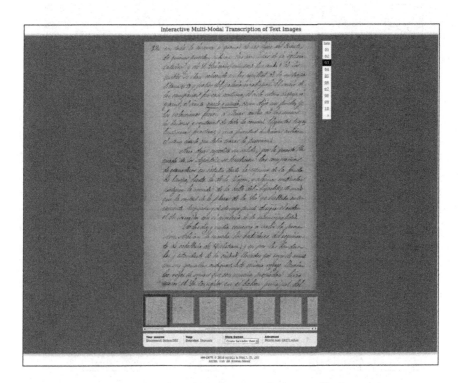

Fig. 6.5 The selected page to be transcribed.

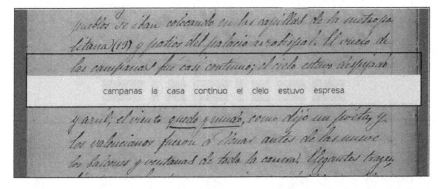

Fig. 6.6 The HTR system proposes a full transcription of the input handwritten text line image.

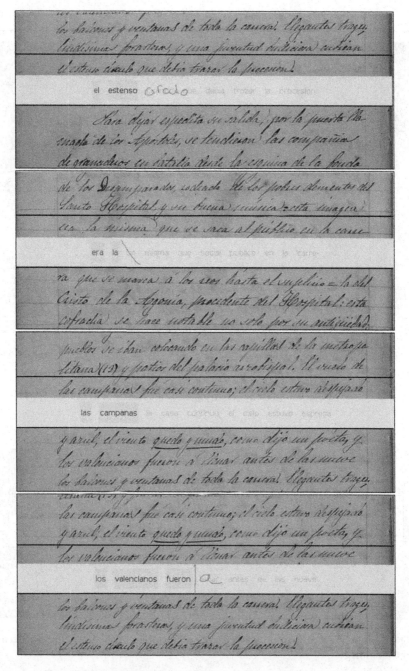

Fig. 6.7   Four interaction gestures to generate and/or validate an error-free prefix.
From top to bottom: substitution, deletion, rejection and insertion.

- Substitution: Place the e-pen over an incorrect word and write down the correct text.
- Deletion: Draw a diagonal line over an incorrect word and it is deleted. The deletion gesture must begin outside the text field boundaries.
- Rejection: By clicking on a word the system proposes a new, most probable suffix where the clicked word has changed.
- Insertion: Draw a vertical line between two words and then write down the text to insert.
- Accept Final Transcription: Draw a verification (v-like) gesture after the last corrected word to accept the full proposed transcription. The next image line will be loaded automatically.

6.3.5 *Keyboard and Mouse Interaction*

If the user prefers, she can works with traditional peripherals like keyboard and mouse. To switch to keyboard mode any key over the application interface must be pressed. It is important to remark that while the stylus pen is moved over the words the focus is updated. So, since the keys work as expected, take these examples when switching to keyboard mode:

- Clicking the space or delete key will delete the text.
- Clicking the TAB key will change to the next word in the tab loop.
- Clicking any alphanumeric or punctuation key will overwrite the word text.
- Clicking non-character keys (UP, CTRL, CAPS, ALT, etc.) will give focus to the current word.

Fig. 6.8 shows an example of the demo in the keyboard interaction mode. The different interactions in the keyboard mode are:

- Substitution: Once the incorrect word has been changed, pressing EN-TER or going to the next word (with the TAB key) the validated prefix will be sent.
- Deletion: Pressing "CTRL + DEL" will delete the selected text field.
- Rejection: this is similar to the "Rejection" presented on the previous subsection, but now using the mouse instead the e-pen. This also can be carried out using the keyboard, pressing "CRTL + UP" the system will propose a new transcription and the previous one will be stored on a internal buffer. Pressing "CRTL + DOWN" will load the previous transcription from the internal buffer.

Fig. 6.8   The keyboard mode.

- Insertion: Pressing the keys "CTRL + SPACE" will insert a new text field to the right of the selected word. If the "SHIFT" key is also pressed, the text field will be inserted to the left of the selected word instead.
- Accept Final Transcription: Pressing "CTRL + ENTER" the full proposed transcription will be accepted. The final transcription will be composed by the words in the text fields until the text field with focus. The next image line will be loaded automatically.

6.4   Evaluation

The empirical tests carried out on previous chapters suggest that, using the MM-CATTI approach, considerable amounts of user effort can be saved with respect to both pure manual work and non-interactive, post-editing processing. While, of course, no definitive conclusions could be derived from these empirical tests, they clearly raised great expectations about the effectiveness and usability of this kind of interactive HTR technology. Therefore, in order to assess whether such expectations were in the right direction, we conducted a preliminary field study that compared the theoretical results with real users working with a CATTI approach or with pure manual work.

6.4.1   *Assessment Measures*

In interactive PR systems the importance of the traditional recognition error rates is diminished, since the intention is to measure how well the user and the system work together. In the tests with real users we have used the WSR measure (introduced in Sec. 4.7.1), which has proven to be useful for estimating the reduction in human effort that can be expected. In addition, we measured the time needed to fully transcribe each page with the different transcription possibilities (manual and CATTI) as well as the residual WER (rWER) after human transcription. The rWER is defined as the WER which remains after the user has typed the transcriptions or corrected/accepted the transcriptions proposed by the system. This value is expected to be greater than zero due to user's errors.

6.4.2   *Corpus*

The corpus used on the experiments was the book partition of the "Cristo-Salvador" (CS), which has been previously presented in Sec. 2.2. To carry out the experiments we used two pages from the test partition of the corpus, most specifically, pages 45 and 46 were used. These pages were selected because they had very similar test-set-based performance metrics (page 45: WER=24.3%, WSR=23.1%; page 46: WER=24.7%, WSR=23.0%) and because they did not entail palaeographical problems, which would require expert knowledge. In Fig. 6.9 we can see the two pages used.

6.4.3   *Participants*

Thirteen participants from our Computer Science department volunteered to cooperate, aged 28 to 61 (M=37.3, 3 females). Most of them were knowledgeable with handwriting transcription tasks, although none was a transcriber expert or had historical knowledge about the book issue. Additionally, only three participants were aware of the existence of a transcription prototype prior to the evaluation.

6.4.4   *Apparatus*

The web-base demonstrator presented in this chapter was modified to carry out the field study. We implemented two HTR engines to assist the document transcription: a trivial manual system and our CATTI system. The user interface (UI) was common to both engines. As previously presented,

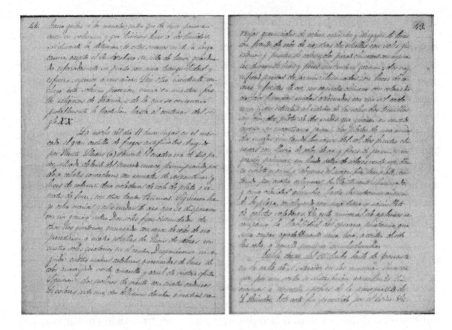

Fig. 6.9   Pages 45 and 46 from the CS corpus.

it provided basic text-editing capabilities, and allowed to transcribe inter-actively each page line by line. The application supported some special editing operations (such as insertions, rejections, or deletions) in order to better assist the user in the transcription process.

Also, a logging mechanism was embedded in the web application. It al-lowed us to register all user interactions in a fine-grained level of detail (e.g., keyboard and mouse events, client/server message exchanging, etc.). The generated log files were reported in XML format for later postprocessing.

6.4.5   *Procedure*

Participants accessed the web-based application via a special URL that were sent to them by email. In order to familiarize with the UI, users informally tested each transcription engine with some test pages, different from the ones reserved for the user-test. Then, people transcribed the two user-test pages; each one with both transcription engines.

It is important to remark that nobody saw these user-test pages before the study. For that reason, it is clear that the engine that were tested first would lead to poorer results — in the next trial users would need less effort in reading the image lines. Thus, to avoid possible biases due to human learnability, the first page (#45) was transcribed with the manual engine first; then the order was inverted for the second page (#46). Finally, participants filled out an online System Usability Scale (SUS) questionnaire [Brooke (1996)] for both systems. Such online form included a text field to allow the users to submit free comments and ideas about their testing experience, as well as giving some insights about possible enhancements and/or related applicability.

6.4.6   *Design*

We carried out a within-subjects repeated measures design. We tested two conditions: transcribing a page with the manual and the CATTI system, taking into account that each one was tested twice — to compensate the above-mentioned learnability bias. We performed a non-parametric test in each case, since normality assumptions did not hold (see below). Additionally, we studied if there were any correlation between trials and between measured variables, for such gathered performance metrics (time, residual WER, and WSR, respectively). We used the R Language [R Development Core Team (2009)] to process the data.

6.5   Results and Discussion

In sum, we can assert that regarding *effectiveness* there are no significant differences, i.e., users can achieve their goals with any of the tested systems. However, it is important to note that, using the CATTI system the obtained rWER is better than using the manual engine. Therefore, the quality of the final transcription is better.

In terms of *efficiency* the CATTI system is the better choice. As expected, the system used firstly to transcribe the pages obtains the worse time, due to the users learning. However, in overall, the time required by a user using the CATTI system is lower than the time using the manual engine.

Regarding to *user satisfaction*, CATTI again seems to be the most preferable option. Now let us delve into a more detailed analysis in order to shed more light to the obtained results. Initially we report the amount and nature of the differences found between both groups. Then we study both the statistically significance and the correlation between the measured variables.

6.5.1　Quantitative Analysis

Tables 6.1 and 6.2 reports the result of the field study. In Table 6.1 we can see the mean and de SD per page for the measured variables, whereas in Table 6.2 the metrics for each participant are shown. We must emphasize that the daily use of any system designed to assist handwriting transcription would involve not having seen previously any of the pages (users usually read a page once and at the same time they just transcribe it).

Table 6.1　Mean (and SD) per page for the measured variables: time (in minutes), rWER & WSR (in %), and differences (in %).

System		Time	rWER	WSR
Overall	Manual	22.2 (3.5)	8.6 (8.2)	97.8 (6.0)
	CATTI	20.6 (3.7)	6.5 (3.7)	30.4 (6.1)
Difference		7.2	24.4	68.9
Page 45	Manual	12.8 (3.5)	12.8 (9.5)	97.3 (7.0)
	CATTI	8.6 (3.2)	7.0 (4.1)	28.6 (4.1)
Difference		32.8	45.3	70.6
Page 46	Manual	9.4 (2.9)	4.1 (2.0)	98.4 (4.6)
	CATTI	12.0 (3.4)	6.0 (3.3)	32.1 (7.1)
Difference		21.6	31.6	67.3

We computed the difference between both systems as diff $= |\frac{m-i}{\max(m,i)}|$, being m and i each measured variable in the manual and interactive versions, respectively.

To determine if data could be assumed to be normally distributed, we run a Shapiro-Wilk normality test [Stephens (1974)]. Given to the results of the normality test (see Fig. 6.11) the data could not be considered normal. We decided thus to use the (non-parametric) two-sample Kolmogorov-Smirnov test for the evaluation study. Additionally, we measured the *probability of improvement* (POI), which estimates if a system is *a priori* better than another for a given user [Bisani and Ney (2004)].

6.5.1.1　Analysis of Time

We observed that, overall, there are no significant differences in transcription times ($D = 0.16$, $p = 0.75$, n.s.). In general, the system used in second place always achieved the best time, because the user already knew the text. The remarkable result is that when the user reads a page in first

Table 6.2   Collected data. Each row holds the metrics for each participant, who is denoted as P##†.

Metric:	Time (s)				rWER (%)				WSR (%)				SUS (%)	
System:	Manual		CATTI		Manual		CATTI		Manual		CATTI		Manual	CATTI
Page|Order:	45|1	46|2	45|2	46|1	45|1	46|2	45|2	46|1	45|1	46|2	45|2	46|1	note‡	
P01	276.3	411.2	463.5	331.9	5.9	2.8	7.0	3.4	100.0	105.5	31.2	25.2	70.0	75.0
P02	514.6	234.1	394.5	243.4	2.4	6.4	4.7	3.2	100.4	92.1	33.7	25.9	62.5	77.5
P03	207.2	336.1	178.0	136.9	9.4	2.4	5.7	2.5	100.4	93.1	38.6	28.2	50.0	37.5
P04	419.6	153.2	250.3	201.0	1.6	18.8	8.5	2.0	100.0	100.0	25.6	28.8	77.5	70.0
P05	319.4	253.0	296.0	249.8	5.1	4.5	2.0	3.8	88.4	100.0	22.6	32.4	77.5	87.5
P06	320.6	218.0	370.4	249.2	3.7	12.8	5.9	5.7	100.4	100.4	22.2	38.2	62.5	97.5
P07	231.6	257.4	201.4	136.2	11.1	3.7	4.9	9.8	101.7	109.4	22.2	29.9	62.5	72.5
P08	461.4	174.2	436.1	315.2	7.8	7.2	10.6	8.6	100.0	86.4	32.4	36.6	52.5	42.5
P09	393.9	380.9	341.2	215.8	12.8	2.8	9.8	14.1	96.5	96.1	33.7	29.4	72.5	90.0
P10	347.8	310.1	224.1	178.7	20.5	11.5	15.3	13.1	100.4	95.4	20.5	33.7	80.0	65.0
P11	218.4	196.8	208.8	190.0	4.1	4.9	9.0	3.4	100.4	88.4	45.6	34.6	65.0	70.0
P12	297.9	189.9	350.4	79.3	4.2	10.2	3.4	2.4	81.6	97.1	30.7	38.2	95.0	62.5
P13	244.2	287.8	342.5	397.1	8.6	2.8	4.5	5.5	105.3	99.5	22.6	27.3	50.0	50.0

Order = 1 means that the user transcribed that page initially with the corresponding engine (inversely, order = 2 means that the user already transcribed the page with the other engine before.)

† In some cases decimals have been padded to better display cell values.

‡ Users only ranked once each system via the online SUS questionnaire, for that reason there are only two SUS columns.

place the chosen engine is not determinant, because one must spend time to accustom to the writing style, interpreting the calligraphy, etc. In this case the POI of CATTI with respect to the manual engine is 53%.

6.5.1.2   *Analysis of rWER*

Overall, CATTI was the best choice regarding to residual WER ($D = 0.11$, $p = 0.99$, n.s.). Although the differences are not statistically significant, the interesting observation is that the results in both pages using CATTI are quite similar, independently of the system used firstly. This is due to the fact that, the hypothesis proposed by the CATTI system can help the user to recognize some of the difficult words of the text. In this case, considering the first time that the user reads a page, the POI of the CATTI engine over the manual engine is 69%.

6.5.1.3   *Analysis of WSR*

Interestingly, the WSR when using the manual engine was below 100%, since there are inherent errors (some users were unable to correctly read all the lines). That means that some users wrote less words in their final transcriptions than they really should have written when using the manual engine. In both conditions CATTI was the best performer, and differences were statistically significant ($D = 1, p < 0.001$). The POI of the CATTI engine regarding the manual engine is 100%. This means that the number of words a user must write and/or correct under the CATTI paradigm is always much lower than with a manual system. Additionally, this fact increases the probability of achieving a high-quality final transcription, since users perform fewer interactions and are prone thus to less errors. It is also interesting to note that, on average, the real WSR achieved by the participants is fairly close to the objective user-test based estimates for the same pages.

6.5.2   *Qualitative Analysis*

Regarding user subjectivity judgement, the SUS scores could be considered normally distributed. Thus, a Welch two-sample t-test was employed to measure the differences between both groups. We observed a clear tendency in favour to CATTI ($t(22) = 0.25$, $p = 0.80$, n.s.), since users generally appreciate the guidance of the CATTI system suggesting partial predictions, given the difficulty of the task proposed in the field study.

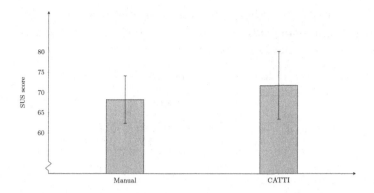

Fig. 6.10 User satisfaction, according to the SUS questionnaire.

Most of the users' comments were alas related to the web UI rather than the transcription engines themselves. Some included *"when clicking on a text field, the whole word is selected"*, *"it is hard to remember some [keyboard] shortcuts"*, or *"a clear and visual user manual would allow not having to learn almost anything before using the system."* Additionally, four users complained about the segmentation of lines, which *"made especially difficult reading those images where words had many ascenders/descenders."* On the other hand, three users noticed that punctuation chars did not contribute to improve predictions in the CATTI system. In fact, they were removed from the language models when training the CATTI engine, since we used bi-grams, and punctuation chars do not notably improve the predictions.

6.5.3 *Correlation Analysis*

We considered significant correlations when the Pearson Coefficient $|r| >$ 0.5 $(r \in [-1, 1])$. Additionally, the Coefficient of Determination $r^2 \in [0, 1]$ allowed us to determine how certain would be a prediction from a given measure.

6.5.3.1 *Correlation between trials*

Overall, CATTI is more stable than the manual engine for all measured variables (see Table 6.3). What is interesting is the consistency between trials for the CATTI engine; no matter if a page has been seen previously or not, CATTI will behave approximately in the same way. However, if the user has seen a page previously, the manual approach will result in less transcription time — although the user will need to write all the words, exposed thus to potentially more errors, and taking into account that this is not a realistic scenario (see Sec. 6.5.1).

Table 6.3   Between-trial Correlation and Determination coefficients.

System	Time r	Time r^2	rWER r	rWER r^2	WSR r	WSR r^2
Manual	-0.29	0.08	-0.22	0.04	-0.001	0
CATTI	0.62	0.38	0.61	0.37	0.63	0.39

6.5.3.2   *Correlation between metrics*

We found a correlation between time and rWER in the manual engine when the page has not been seen previously: $r = -0.615$ ($r^2 = 0.37$). For the same engine, rWER and WSR seem to have a relative influence on the user subjective ratings: $r = 0.45$ ($r^2 = 0.20$); $r = -0.75$ ($r^2 = 0.57$). This fact reinforced our initial hypothesis. For the CATTI engine we did not observed relevant between-metrics correlations.

6.5.4   *Limitations of the Study*

There are a number of reasons why we were unfortunately not able to achieve statistically significant differences between the tested engines in some cases. First, the limited size of the user sample was a primary factor of influence. Taking also into account that users were not experts in transcribing ancient documents, a dispersed behaviour was expected (i.e., some users were considerably faster/slower than others, see Table 6.2 and Fig. 6.11). Second, the pages were really deteriorated, making more difficult the reading for the users. For that reason, there is a great difference between the first time that a user had to transcribe a page and the subsequent attempts. Third, most of the participants had never faced neither any of the implemented engines nor the web UI before the study, so it is expected a logical learning curve prior to using such systems in a daily basis. A simplified starting level would minimize this effect for the task; however we tried to select a scenario as close as possible to a realistic setting. Finally, the web interface was just a prototype, and it is well known that a careful design of the UI is a primary factor to tap the possibilities of the CATTI technology. However, despite of the above mentioned limitations, there is a comprehensible bias in favour of the CATTI paradigm over the manual system.

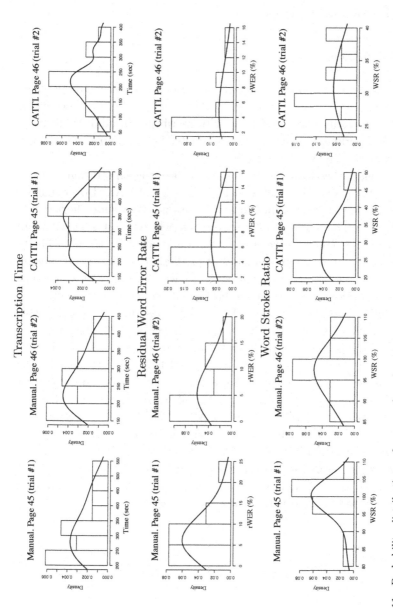

Fig. 6.11 Probability distributions of measured performance metrics between users. Outer columns allow to compare both systems when transcribing a page for the first time (Vice versa for the inner columns.) Notice how gathered data could not be considered normally distributed in most cases.

Additionally, as observed, the probability of improvement of an CATTI engine over manual transcription revealed that the interactive-predictive paradigm worked better for all users.

6.6 Conclusions

The results of the automatic evaluation metrics discussed in the previous chapters were intended to give us a rough idea of how the system could be *expected* to perform when used by real transcribers. In addition to these laboratory experiments, the prototype presented in this chapter has allowed us to carry out tests with real users.

According to these tests, the system does meet the expectations derived from the laboratory experiments. The advantage of CATTI over manual transcription seems clear, although it goes beyond the human effort reductions achieved. The proposed interactive approach constitutes a much more natural way of producing correct text. With and adequate UI, CATTI lets the users be dynamically in command: if predictions are not good enough, then the user simply keeps typing at her own pace; otherwise, she can accept (partial) predictions, thereby saving both thinking and typing effort.

In addition informal tests carried out with users using MM-CATTI with a touch screen have shown that the on-line HTR feedback decoding accuracy also meet the expected results. Even though the on-line HTR HMMs were trained from artificially built words using UNIPEN character samples, the accuracy in real operation with real users is observed to be similar to that shown in the laboratory results. It also follows from the tests that the interactive scenario implemented in the MM-CATTI server is really more comfortable and friendlier to the user than plain post-editing.

Future work includes incorporating some of the modifications and enhancements that users insightfully reported at the end of our study. Thus, a much more extensive and large-scale evaluation of the CATTI paradigm will be ready to be tested with professional transcribers.

Chapter 7

Conclusions and Outlook

7.1 Conclusions

In this book, we have presented a new interactive approach to the transcription of handwritten documents, which combines the efficiency of automatic HTR systems with the accuracy of users. This approach is based on a recently introduced framework called "interactive predictive processing" [Vidal *et al.* (2007b)]. We have called this approach "Computer Assisted Transcription of Text Images" (CATTI). Here, the corrections made by a human transcriber become part of a prefix of the final target transcription. This prefix is used by CATTI to suggest a new suffix that the human transcriber can accept or modify in an iterative way until a satisfactory, correct target transcription is finally produced. Empirical tests presented in this book clearly support the benefits of using this approach rather than traditional HTR followed by human post-editing.

Two different CATTI implementations have been studied. The first consists in dynamically building a special language model and the second one in more sophisticated word-graph techniques. In the word-graph based implementation, efficient error-correcting parsing algorithms have been adapted, implemented and integrated in order to guarantee low response time while preserving adequately accurate transcription suggestions.

In order to improve the ergonomy of CATTI, the use system the use of Pointer Actions (PA) as an additional information source has been also considered. In this scenario, as soon as the user points out the place where the next error is found, the system proposes a new, hopefully more correct, continuation, thereby trying to anticipate up-coming user corrections. Obtained results show that a significant benefit can be obtained, in terms of expected effort reductions. It is worth noting that alternative (n-best) suffixes could also be obtained with the conventional CATTI system. However, by considering the rejected words to propose the alternative suffixes, the PA interaction method is more effective and seems more comfortable for the user.

Furthering the goal of making the interaction process friendlier to the user, character-level interaction has been studied. Considering the results obtained in the experiments, we can conclude that using this interaction level not only allows for more ergonomic and friendly interfaces, but significant amounts of human effort in the handwritten text transcription process can be saved. It is worth noting, however, that results obtained at the character and word levels are not directly comparable, and future work is needed to better assess the relative advantages of word and character-level interaction.

We have also studied the use of on-line touch-screen handwritten pen strokes as a complementary means to input the required CATTI corrective feedback. We call this multimodal approach "MM-CATTI". From the results, we observe that the use of this more ergonomic feedback modality comes at the cost of only a reasonably small number of additional interaction steps needed to correct the few feedback decoding errors. The number of these extra steps is kept very small thanks to the MM-CATTI ability to use interaction-derived constraints to considerably improve the on-line HTR feedback decoding accuracy. Clearly, this would have not been possible if just a conventional, off-the-shelf on-line HTR decoder were trivially used for the correction steps.

The advantage of CATTI and MM-CATTI over traditional HTR followed by post-editing goes beyond the good estimates of human effort reductions achieved. When difficult transcription tasks with high WER are considered, expert users generally refuse to post-edit conventional HTR output. In contrast, the proposed interactive approaches constitute a much more natural way of producing correct text. With an adequate user interface, CATTI or MM-CATTI let the users be dynamically in command: If predictions are not good enough, then the user simply keeps typing at his/her own pace; otherwise, he/she can accept (partial) predictions and thereby save both thinking and typing effort.

In addition to the laboratory experiments reported in chapters 3-5, a complete MM-CATTI prototype has been implemented and already submitted to preliminary, informal tests with real users (Chap. 6). According to these tests, the system does meet the expectations derived from the laboratory experiments.

7.2 Outlook

A potential problem with the use of MM-CATTI in practice can arise when transcribing documents for which an adequate full lexicon cannot be established beforehand (often referred to as open-vocabulary operation). Following the tradition in Automatic Speech Recognition (ASR), in order to facilitate comparations and reproducibility, all the MM-CATTI experiments here reported have been carried out under the closed-vocabulary assumption. However, practical transcription tasks typically entail open-vocabulary operation and some solution to this problem is needed. Of course, the lexicon of a task need not be strictly limited to the word-forms found in the (training) data available of this task. In practice, dictionaries or texts from other similar tasks or documents are often used to expand the word-forms found in the training data of the task considered. But some amount of residual out-of-vocabulary (OOV) word-forms must be expected. Furthermore, this can be really important in the case of ancient documents (one of the main MM-CATTI targets) where, for example, OOV words appear because of the frequent use of abbreviations/acronyms, which change from one era to another and even from one document to another [Romero *et al.* (2010)]. Thanks to the interactive nature of MM-CATTI operation, a simple way to cope with this problem is to progressively enrich the given lexicon by successively incorporating all the OOV tokens which appear in the document being processed [Serrano and Juan (2010)]. This way, a user correction will only be needed the first time a new word or abbreviation appears; later appearances will hopefully be correctly recognized by the system.

This can be seen as one of the simplest forms of *adaptive learning*, which is one of the main future research topics we plan to explore in the context of MM-CATTI. The correct transcriptions that are being continuously produced during the interactive work, can be advantageously used to dynamically and adaptively improve the underlying language and morphological off-line HTR models of the task or document(s) considered. In speech recognition, well known Adaptive Learning techniques exist for adapting the acoustic HMM models to the speaker and/or the audio channel (see for example [Leggetter and Woodland (1995); Woodland (2001); Welling *et al.* (2002); Pitz and Ney (2005)]). These techniques are currently in use in many state-of-the-art recognition systems. In addition, Language Model adaptation is also possible ([Kuhn and Mori (1990); Bellegarda (2004); L. Nepveu and Foster (2004); Serrano *et al.* (2010); Serrano and

Juan (2010)]). In traditional ASR systems, these techniques require the user to provide adequate amounts of adaptation data, which is not always possible, convenient or cost-effective. Typically, only small quantities of adaptation data can be used, which results in the systems not being able to take full advantage of adaptation techniques. In CATTI operation, perfectly supervised adaptation data is being produced continuously, without the user even being aware of their production.

Similarly, the MM-CATTI feedback decoding accuracy can be easily (and significantly) improved by adaptively retraining the on-line HTR morphology HMMs with the real pen-strokes which are being continuously produced by the specific user who is interacting with the system.

As explained in Chap. 4, the interaction between users and the CATTI system is not necessarily restricted to the recognition module. As a future work, a more general approach where the user can also interact with the preprocessing module in order to help correcting segmentation or preprocessing errors will be studied. The system could then use these corrections to improve the recognition accuracy. Following these ideas, there are some recent works [Ramos Terrades *et al.* (2010); Terrades *et al.* (2010)] addressing interactive-predictive approaches applied to layout analysis. In this case, new assessment measures that take into account all the number of actions needed by the user in order to start from a digitized document and produce correct transcriptions will be defined.

Finally, our plans for future work include to carry out formal and extensive field tests to assess the validity of our assumptions and estimations under real working conditions of expert (paleography) transcribers of handwritten (historic) documents. These experiments should be similar to those conducted in [Casacuberta *et al.* (2009)] for Computer Assisted Translation (CAT), where the results showed that suffix-predictive Interactive Machine Translation systems can allow translators to increase their productivity while maintaining high-quality.

Acknowledgements

Work supported by the Spanish Government (MICINN and "Plan E") under the MITTRAL (TIN2009-14633-C03-01) research project and under the research programme Consolider Ingenio 2010: MIPRCV (CSD2007-00018).

Appendix A

Symbols and Acronyms

A.1 Symbols

$\Pr(\ldots)$	the unkwnown "true" probability.
$P(\ldots)$	the model probability.
a_{ij}	estate transition probabitity on an HMM from the state q_i to the state q_j: $a_{ij} \equiv a(q_i, q_j)$.
$b_i(x)$	emission vector x probability distribution function on an HMM for the state q_i : $b_i(x) \equiv b(q_i, x)$.
G	number of Gaussians on a mixture.
g	index for the Gaussians on a mixture.
μ_{jg}	mean vector for the component g in the Gaussian mixture of the state q_j on a HMM.
Σ_{jg}	covariance matrix for the component g in the Gaussian mixture of the state q_j on a HMM.
c_{jg}	weighting coefficient for the component g in the Gaussian mixture of the state q_j on a HMM.
$\mathbf{x} = x_1, x_2, \ldots$	a sequence of feature vectors.
x_i and $\vec{x}_i$	the feature vector i of the sequence $\mathbf{x}$.
M	number of feature vectors on the sequence $\mathbf{x}$.
$\mathbf{x}_i^j$	subsequence of feature vectors extracted of the sequence $\mathbf{x}$, formed by the frames between the position i and j inclusive.
$\mathbf{w} = w_1, w_2, \ldots$	sequence of words.
w_i	ith word in the word sequence $\mathbf{w}$.
l	number of words in the sequence $\mathbf{w}$.
$\mathbf{w}_i^j$	a word subsequence extracted of the sequence $\mathbf{w}$, formed by the words between the position i and j inclusive.

$N \times M$	number of cells in which is divided the handwritten text image. N is the number of rows and M is the number of columns or frames.
$r \times s$	number of cells in the analysis windows to obtain smoothed values of the studied features. r is the number of rows and s is the number of columns.
$n \times m$	number of pixels on the analysis windows. n is the number of rows and m is the number of columns.
e	an edge of a word graph.
$\omega(e)$	word associated with the edge e on a word graph.
q	a node on a word graph.
$t(q)$	horizontal position of the handwritten image that corresponds with the node q on a word graph.
$p(e)$	probability of the edge e on a word graph.
$\varphi(e)$	score of the edge e on a word graph.
$\phi = e_1, e_2, \ldots, e_M$	a path of states on a word graph.
$S(h)$	score of the path h.
$d(\mathbf{w})$	set of paths on a word graph that produce the sequence $\mathbf{w}$.
$\phi_{\mathbf{w}}$	one of the paths of $d(\mathbf{w})$.
$\mathbf{p'}$	validated prefix of the transcription hypothesis which is error free.
v	a word of the vocabulary task.
$\mathbf{p}$	new validated prefix of the transcription hypothesis ($\mathbf{p'}$ plus v).
$\mathbf{s}$	possible suffix that follows the validated prefix $\mathbf{p}$.
b	point that divide the sequence $\mathbf{x}$ into two partes, prefix and suffix.
Q_p	set of states on a word graphs that define paths from the initial state whose associated word sequence is p.
α	grammar scale factor.
β	word insertion penalty.
(x_t, y_t)	point of the trajectory of the pen-stroke.

x'_t and y'_t	fist derivatives of the point (x_t, y_t).
x''_t and y''_t	second derivatives of the point (x_t, y_t).
k_t	Curvature. The inverse of the local raius of the trajectori in each point.
c	class label.
M_c	a HMM for the chatacter class c.
l_c	average lenght of the sequence of feature vectors used to train M_c.
f	state load factor. Measures the average number of feature vectors modelled per state.
N_S	number of states on the HMMs.
N_{Sc}	number of states for the HMM character class M_c.
N_G	number of gaussians on the HMMs.
γ	weighted coefficient of the penalization due to the number of different characters between words.
e	a word transcription error.
m	a mouse action.
c	a character sequence.
p"	part of the validated prefix formed by completed words.
v_p	prefix of a word.
v_s	suffix of a word.
s'	part of the suffix formed by completed words.
t	a sequence of real value vectors representing on-line touchscreen pen strokes.
κ	a keystroke.
d	a word representing the decoding of t.

A.2 Acronyms

AJAX	Asyncronous JavaScript And XML
API	Application ProgrammingInterface
ASR	Automatic Speech Recognition
BIVALDI	Biblioteca Valenciana Digital
CATTI	Computer Assisted Transcription of Handwritten Text Images
CER	Character Error Rate
CL-CATTI	CATTI at character level
CS	Cristo Salvador
ECP	Error Correcting Penalty
EER	Estimated Effort Reduction
EM	Expectation Maximisation
ER	Classification Error Rate
FKI	Research Group on computer Vision and Artificial Inteligence
FSM	Finite State Machine
FS	Finite State
GSF	Grammar Scale Factor
HMM	Hidden Markov Model
HTR	Handwritten Text Recognition
IAM	Institute of Computer Science and Applied Mathematics
IAMDB	IAM Handwriting Database
IP	Interative Predictive
IPP	Interactive Predictive Processing
IPR	Interactive Pattern Recognition
KSR	Key Stroke Ratio
LOB	Lancaster-Oslo/Bergen
MA	Mouse Action
MM-CATTI	Multimodal Computer Assisted Transcription of Handwritten Text Images
NN	Nearest Neighbour
OCR	Optical Character Recognition
ODEC	Spontaneous Handwritten Paragraphs Corpus
OOV	Out Of Vocabulary
PA-CATTI	CATTI using Pointer Actions
PAR	Pointer Action Rate
PKSR	Post-editing Key Stroke Ratio

PR	Pattern Recognition
REA	Recursive Enumeration Algorithm
RLSA	Run-Length Smoothing Algorithm
SFSA	Stochastic Finite State Automation
WDAG	Weighted Directed Acyclic Graph
WER	Word Error Rate
WG	Word Graph
WIP	Word Insertion Penalty
WSR	Word Stroke Ratio

Bibliography

Ahmad, A. R., Khalia, M., Viard-Gaudin, C. and Poisson, E. (2004). Online handwriting recognition using support vector machine, in *The Proceedings of TENCON. IEEE Region 10 Conference*, Vol. A, pp. 311–314.

Alabau, V., Ortiz, D., Romero, V. and Ocampo, J. (2009). A multimodal predictive-interactive application for computer assisted transcription and translation, in *Proceedings of the International Conference on Multimodal Interfaces* (ACM, New York, NY, USA), ISBN 978-1-60558-772-1, pp. 227–228, doi:http://doi.acm.org/10.1145/1647314.1647358.

Amengual, J. C. and Vidal, E. (1998). Efficient Error-Corecting Viterbi Parsing, *IEEE Transactions on Pattern Analysis and Machine Intelligence* **20**, 10, pp. 1109–1116.

Amin, A. and Ficher, S. (2000). A document skew detection method using the hough transform. *Pattern Analysis and Applications* **3**, pp. 243–253.

Barrachina, S., Bender, O., Casacuberta, F., Civera, J., Cubel, E., Khadivi, S., Lagarda, A. L., Ney, H., Tomás, J. and Vidal, E. (2009). Statistical approaches to computer-assisted translation, *Computational Linguistics* **35**, 1, pp. 3–28.

Bazzi, I., Schwartz, R. and Makhoul, J. (1999). An Omnifont Open-Vocabulary OCR System for English and Arabic, *IEEE Transactions on Pattern Analysis and Machine Intelligence* **21**, 6, pp. 495–504.

Bellegarda, J. (2004). Statistical language model adaptation: Rewiew and perspectives, *Speech communication* **42**, 1, pp. 93–108.

Berger, A. L., Pietra, V. J. D. and Pietra, S. A. D. (1996). A maximum entropy approach to natural language processing, *Computational Linguistics* **22**, pp. 39–71, URL http://portal.acm.org/citation.cfm?id=234285.234289.

Bertolami, R. and Bunke, H. (2008). Hidden markov model-based ensemble methods for offline handwritten text line recognition, *Pattern Recognition* **41**, 11, pp. 3452–3460.

Bisani, M. and Ney, H. (2004). Bootstrap estimates for confidence intervals in ASR performance evaluation, in *Proceedings of International Conference on Acoustics, Speech, and Signal Processing*, pp. 409–12.

Bozinovic, R. and Srihari, S. (1989). Off-line cursive script word recognition,

IEEE Transactions on Pattern Analysis and Machine Intelligence **11**, 1, pp. 68–83.

Brakensiek, A., Rottland, J., Kosmala, A. and Rigoll, G. (2000). Off-Line Handwriting Recognition Using Various Hybrid Modeling Techniques and Character N-Grams, in *7th International Workshop on Frontiers in Handwriting Recognition* (Amsterdam, The Netherlands), pp. 343–352.

Brooke, J. (1996). SUS: A "quick and dirty" usability scale, in *Usability Evaluation in Industry* (Taylor and Francis).

Bunke, H. (2003). Recognition of cursive roman handwriting- past, present and future, in *Proceedings of the 7th International Conference Document Analysis and Recognition* (IEEE Computer Society, Washington, DC, USA), p. 448.

Bunke, H., Roth, M. and Suchakat-Talamazzini, E. (1995). Off-line cursive handwriting recognition using hidden markov models, *Pattern Recognition* **28**, 9, pp. 1399–1413.

Cao, Y., Wang, S. and Li, H. (2003). Skew detection and correction in document images based on straiht-line fitting, *Pattern Recognition Letters* **24**, pp. 1871–1879.

Casacuberta, F., Civera, J., Cubel, E., Lagarda, A., Lapalme, G., Macklovitch, E. and Vidal, E. (2009). Human interaction for high quality machine translation, *Communications of the ACM* **52**, 10, pp. 135–138.

Casacuberta, F. and de la Higuera, C. (2000). Computational complexity of problems on probabilistic grammars and transducers, in *Proceedings of the 5th International Colloquium on Grammatical Inference* (Springer-Verlag, London, UK), ISBN 3-540-41011-2, pp. 15–24.

Civera, J., Vilar, J., Cubel, E., Lagarda, A., Barrachina, S., Casacuberta, F., Vidal, E., Picó, D. and González, J. (2004a). A syntactic pattern recognition approach to computer assisted translation, in *Advances in Statistical, Structural and Syntactical Pattern Recognition*, Lecture Notes in Computer Science (Springer-Verlag).

Civera, J., Vilar, J. M., Cubel, E., Lagarda, A. L., Barrachina, S., Vidal, E., Casacuberta, F., Picó, D. and González, J. (2004b). From machine translation to computer assisted translation using finite-state models, in *Proceedings of the 2004 Conference on Empirical Methods in Natural Language Processing* (Barcelona).

Dimauro, G., Impedovo, S., Modugno, R. and Pirlo, G. (2002). A new database for research on bank-check processing, in *8th International Workshop on Frontiers in Handwriting Recognition*, pp. 524–528.

Drida, F. (2006). Towards restoring historic documents degraded over time, in *Proceedings of the Second International conference on Document Image Analysis for Libraries*, IEEE Computer Society (Washington, DC, USA), pp. 350–357.

Duda, R. O. and Hart, P. E. (1973). *Pattern Classification and Scene Analysis* (J. Wiley and Sons).

El-Yacoubi, A., Guilloux, M., Sabourin, R. and Suem, C. Y. (1999). An hmm-based approach for off-line unconstrained handwritten word modeling and recognition. *IEEE Transactions on Pattern Analysis and Machine Intelligence* **21**, 8, pp. 752–760.

España Boquera, S., Castro-Bleda, M., Gorbe-Moya, J. and Zamora-Martinez, F. (2011). Improving offline handwritten text recognition with hybrid hmm/ann models, *IEEE Transactions on Pattern Analysis and Machine Intelligence* **33**, 4, pp. 767 –779, doi:10.1109/TPAMI.2010.141.

Francis, W. and Kucera, H. (1964). *Manual of Information to Accompany a Standard Corpus of Present-Day Edited American English, for use with Digital Computers.*, Department of Linguistics, Brown University, Providence, Rhode Island, USA.

Garsid, R., Leech, G. and Váradi, T. (1995). *Manual of Information for the Lancaster Parsed Corpus*, Bergen, Norway: Norwegian Computing Center for the Humanities.

Giménez, A., Khoury, I. and Juan, A. (2010). Windowed Bernoulli Mixture HMMs for Arabic Handwritten Word Recognition, in *Proceedings of the 12th International Conference on Frontiers in Handwriting Recognition* (Kolkata (India)).

Graves, A., Liwicki, M., Fernandez, S., Bertolami, R., Bunke, H. and Schmidhuber, J. (2009). A novel connectionist system for unconstrained handwriting recognition, *IEEE Transactions on Pattern Analysis and Machine Intelligence* **31**, 5, pp. 855 –868, doi:10.1109/TPAMI.2008.137.

Guyon, I., Schomaker, L., Plamondon, R., Liberman, M. and Janet, S. (1994). UNIPEN Project of On-Line Data Exchange and Recognizer Benchmarks, in *Proceedings of the 14th International Conference on Pattern Recognition* (Jerusalem (Israel)), pp. 29–33.

Holmes, J., Vine, B. and Johnson, G. (1998). *Guide to the Wellington Corpus of Spoken New Zealand English*, School of Linguistics and Applied Language Studies, Victoria University of Wellington, Wellington, New Zealand.

Huang, B. Q., Zhang, Y. B. and Kechadi, M. T. (2007). Preprocessing techniques for online handwriting recognition, in *Proceedings of the Seventh International Conference on Intelligent Systems Design and Applications* (IEEE Computer Society, Washington, DC, USA), ISBN 0-7695-2976-3, pp. 793–800.

Impedovo, S., Ottaviano, L. and Occhiegro, S. (1991). Optical character recognition a survey, *International Journal of Pattern Recognition and Artificial Intelligence* **5**, 1, pp. 1–24.

Jaeger, S., Manke, S., Reichert, J. and Waibel, A. (2001). On-Line Handwriting Recognition: The NPen++ Recognizer, *International Journal on Document Analysis and Recognition* **3**, 3, pp. 169–181.

Jelinek, F. (1998). *Statistical Methods for Speech Recognition* (MIT Press).

Jiménez, V. M. and marzal, A. (1999). Computing the k shortest paths: a new algorithm and an experimental coparison, in J. S. Viter and C. D. Zaraliagis (eds.), *Algorithm Engineering, Lecture Notes in Computer Science (LNCS)*, Vol. 1668 (Springer-Verlag), pp. 15–29.

Johansson, S., Leech, G. and Goodluck, H. (1978). *Manual of Information to Accompany the Lancaster-Oslo/bergen Corpus of British English, for Use with Digital Computers*, Department of English, University of Oslo, Norway.

Juan, A. and Vidal, E. (2001). On the use of Bernoulli mixture models for text classification, in *Proceedings of the Workshop on Pattern Recognition in Information Systems* (Setúbal (Portugal)).

Katz, S. M. (1987). Estimation of Probabilities from Sparse Data for the Language Model Component of a Speech Recognizer, *IEEE Transactions on Acoustics, Speech and Signal Processing* **ASSP-35**, pp. 400–401.

Kavallieratou, E., Fakotakis, N. and Kokkinaki, G. (2002). An unconstrained handwriting recognition system, *International Journal of Document Analysis and Recognition* **4**, pp. 226–242.

Kavallieratou, E. and Stamatatos, E. (2006). Improving the quality of degraded document images, in *Proceedings of the Second International Conference on Document Image Analysis for Libraries* (IEEE Computer Society, Washington, DC, USA), ISBN 0-7695-2531-8, pp. 340–349, doi: http://dx.doi.org/10.1109/DIAL.2006.23.

Keysers, D., Paredes, R., Ney, H. and Vidal, E. (2002). Combination of tangent vectors and local representations for handwritten digit recognition, in *International Workshop on Statistical Pattern Recognition*, Lecture Notes in Computer Science (Springer-Verlag), pp. 407–441.

Kim, G., Govindaraju, V. and Srihari, S. (1999). An architecture for handwritten text recognition systems, *International Journal of Document Analysis and Recognition* **2**, 1, pp. 37–44.

Kneser, R. and Ney, H. (1995). Improved backing-off for m-gram language modeling, (IEEE Computer Society, Los Alamitos, CA, USA), ISBN 0-7803-2431-5, pp. 181–184, doi:http://doi.ieeecomputersociety.org/10.1109/ICASSP.1995.479394.

Koerich, A. L., Sabourin, R. and Suens, C. Y. (2003). Large vocabulary off-line handwriting recognition: A survey, *Pattern Analysis Applications* **6**, 2, pp. 97–121.

Kuhn, R. and Mori, R. D. (1990). A cache-based natural language model for speech recognition, *IEEE Transactions on Pattern Analysis and machine Intelligence* **12**, 6, pp. 570–583.

L. Nepveu, G. L., P. Langlais and Foster, G. H. (2004). Adaptive language and translation models for interactive machine translation, in *Proceedings of the 2004 Conference on Empirical Methods in Natural Language Processing* (Barcelona, Spain), pp. 190–197.

Lee, K.-F. (1989). Automatic speech recognition: The development of the sphinx system, *Kluwer Academic Publishers, Boston/Dordrecht/London* .

Lee, S. W. (1996). Off-line recognition of totally unconstrained handwritten numerals using mcnn, *IEEE Transactions on Pattern Analysis and Machine Intelligence* **18**, pp. 648–652.

Leggetter, C. J. and Woodland, P. C. (1995). Maximum likelihood linear regression for speaker adaptation of continuous density hidden markov models, *Computer Speech and Language* **9**, 2, pp. 171–185.

Liu, P. and Soong, F. K. (2006). Word graph based speech recognition error correction by handwriting input, in *Proceedings of the 8th international conference on Multimodal Interfaces* (ACM, New York, NY, USA), ISBN 1-59593-541-X, pp. 339–346.

Llobet, R., Navarro-Cerdan, J. R., Perez-Cortes, J.-C. and Arlandis, J. (2010). Ocr post-processing using weighted finite-state transducers, in *Proceedings of the 12th International Conference on Frontiers in Handwriting Recognition* (Kolkata (India)), pp. 2021–2024.

Lowerre, B. T. (1976). *The harpy speech recognition system*, Ph.D. thesis, Carnegie mellon University, Pittsburgh, PA, USA.

Manke, S., Finke, M. and Waibel, A. (????). Npen++: A writer independent, large vocabulary on-line cursive handwriting recognition system, in *International Conference on Document Analysis and Recogniton* (Montreal).

Marti, U.-V. and Bunke, H. (1999). A full English sentence database for off-line handwriting recognition, in *Proceedings of the International Conference Document Analysis and Recognition* (Bangalore (India)), pp. 705–708.

Marti, U.-V. and Bunke, H. (2001). Using a Statistical Language Model to improve the preformance of an HMM-Based Cursive Handwriting Recognition System, *International Journal of Pattern Recognition and Artificial Intelligence* **15**, 1, pp. 65–90.

Marti, U.-V. and Bunke, H. (2002). The iam-database: an english sentence database for off-line handwriting recognition, *International Journal on Document Analysis and Recognition* **5**, pp. 39–46.

Mori, S., Suen, C. Y. and Yamamoto, K. (1992). Historial review of ocr research and development, *Proceedings of the IEEE* **80**, 7, pp. 1029–1058.

Morita, M., Facon, J., Bortolozzi, F., Garnes, S. and Saboruin., R. (1999). Mathematical morphology and weighted least squares to correct handwriting baseline skew. in *Proceedings of the 5th International Conference on Document Analysis and Recognition*, Vol. 1, pp. 430–433.

Ney, H., Essen, U. and Kneser, R. (1994). On struturing probabilistic dependencies in stochastic language modeling, *Computer speech and Language* **8**, 1, pp. 1–28.

Ogawa, A., Takeda, K. and Itakura, F. (1998). Balancing acoustic and linguistic probabilites, in *Proceeding IEEE Conference Acoustics, Speech, and Signal Processing*, Vol. 1.

Ortmanns, S., Ney, H. and Aubert, X. (1997). A word graph algorithm for large vocabulary continuous speech recognition, *Computer Speech and Language* **11**, 1, pp. 43 – 72, doi:DOI:10.1006/csla.1996.0022, URL http://www.sciencedirect.com/science/article/B6WCW-45N4RJB-N/2/0f22c5b07ee9378da100a928907910e7.

Parizeau, M., Lemieux, A. and Gagn, C. (2001). Character Recognition Experiments using Unipen Data, in *Proceedings of the Sixth International Conference on Document Analysis and Recognition*, ISBN 0-7695-1263-1, pp. 481–485.

Pastor, M. (2007). *Aportaciones al reconocimiento automático de texto manuscrito*, Ph.D. thesis, Departament de Sistemes Informàtics i Computació, València, Spain, advisors: E. Vidal and A.H. Tosselli.

Pastor, M., Toselli, A. and Vidal, E. (2004). Projection profile based algorithm for slant removal, in *International Conference on Image Analysis and Recognition*, Lecture Notes in Computer Science (Springer-Verlag, Porto, Portugal), pp. 183–190.

Pastor, M., Toselli, A. H., Romero, V. and Vidal, E. (2006). Improving handwritten off-line text slant correction, in *Proccedings of The Sixth IASTED international Conference on Visualization, Imaging, and Image Processing* (Palma de Mallorca, Spain).

Pastor, M., Toselli, A. H. and Vidal, E. (2005a). Writing speed normalization for on-line handwritten text recognition, in *Eighth International Conference on Document Analysis and Recognition, Lecture Notes in Computer Science*, Vol. II (IEEE Computer Society, Seul (Korea)), ISBN 0-7695-2420-6, pp. 1131–1135.

Pastor, M., Toselli, A. H. and Vidal, E. (2005b). Writing Speed Normalization for On-Line Handwritten Text Recognition, in *Proceedings of the Eighth International Conference on Document Analysis and Recognition* (Seoul, Korea), pp. 1131–1135.

Pérez-Cortes, J. C., Amengual, J.-C., Arlandis, J. and Llobet, R. (2000). Stochastic error-correcting parsing for ocr post-processing, in *International Conference on Pattern Recognition*, pp. 4405–4408.

Pitz, M. and Ney, H. (2005). Vocal tract normalization equals linear transformation in cepstral space, *IEEE Transactions on Speech and Audio Processing* **13**, 5, pp. 930–944.

Plamondon, R. and Srihari, S. N. (2000). On-Line and Off-Line Handwriting Recognition: A Comprehensive Survey, *IEEE Transactions on Pattern Analysis and Machine Intelligence* **22**, 1, pp. 63–84.

Plötz, T. and Fink, G. A. (2009). Markov models for offline handwriting recognition: a survey, *International Journal on Document Analisys and Recognition* **12**, pp. 269–298, doi:http://dx.doi.org/10.1007/s10032-009-0098-4, URL http://dx.doi.org/10.1007/s10032-009-0098-4.

R Development Core Team (2009). *R: A language and environment for statistical computing* (R Foundation for Statistical Computing, Vienna, Austria), ISBN 3-900051-07-0.

Rabiner, L. (1989). A Tutorial of Hidden Markov Models and Selected Application in Speech Recognition, *Proceedings IEEE* **77**, pp. 257–286.

Rabiner, L. R. and Juang, B. H. (1993). *Fundamentals of Speech Recognition* (Prentice-Hall, Englewood Cliffs, New Jersey, USA).

Ramos Terrades, O., Serrano, N., Gordó, A., Valveny, E. and Juan, A. (2010). Interactive-predictive detection of handwritten text blocks, in *Document Recognition and Retrieval XVII*, Vol. 7534, doi:10.1117/12.839665.

Ratzlaff, E. H. (2003). Methods, Report and Survey for the Comparison of Diverse Isolated Character Recognition Results on the UNIPEN Database, in *Proceedings of the Seventh International Conference on Document Analysis and Recognition*, Vol. 1 (Edinburgh, Scotland), pp. 623–628.

Rodríguez, L., Casacuberta, F. and Vidal, E. (2007). Computer Assisted Speech Transcription, in *Proceedings of the third Iberian Conference on Pattern*

Recognition and Image Analysis, Lecture Notes in Computer Science, Vol. 4477 (Girona (Spain)), pp. 241–248.

Romero, V. (2010). *Multimodal Interactive Transcription of Handwritten Text Images,* Ph.D. thesis, Departamento de Sistemas Informáticos y Computación. Universidad Politécnica de Valencia, Valencia (Spain), advisor(s): Dr. E. Vidal and Dr. A. H. Toselli.

Romero, V., Alabau, V. and Benedí, J. M. (2007a). Combination of N-grams and Stochastic Context-Free Grammars in an Offline Handwritten Recognition System, in *3rd Iberian Conference on Pattern Recognition and Image Analysis, LNCS,* Vol. 4477 (Springer-Verlag, Girona (Spain)), pp. 467–474.

Romero, V., Giménez, A. and Juan, A. (2007b). Explicit Modelling of Invariances in Bernoulli Mixtures for Binary Images, in *3rd Iberian Conference on Pattern Recognition and Image Analysis, Lecture Notes in Computer Science,* Vol. 4477 (Springer-Verlag, Girona (Spain)), pp. 539–546.

Romero, V., Leiva, L., Alabau, V., Toselli, A. and Vidal, E. (2009a). A web-based demo to interactive multimodal transcription of historic text images, in *Proocedings of the 13th european conference on digital libraries, LNCS,* Vol. 5714 (Corfu, Greece), pp. 459–460.

Romero, V., Levia, L. A., Toselli, A. H. and Vidal, E. (2009b). Interactive multimodal transcription of text imagse using a web-based demo system, in *Procedings of the International Conference on Intelligent User Interfaces* (Sanibel Island, Florida), pp. 477–478.

Romero, V., Pastor, M., Toselli, A. H. and Vidal, E. (2006). Criteria for handwritten off-line text size normalization, in *Proceedings of The Sixth IASTED international Conference on Visualization, Imaging, and Image Processing* (Palma de Mallorca, Spain).

Romero, V., Toselli, A. H., Civera, J. and Vidal, E. (2008). Improvements in the computer assisted transciption system of handwritten text images, in *8th International Workshop on Pattern Recognition in Information Systems* (Barcelona (Spain)), pp. 103–112.

Romero, V., Toselli, A. H., Rodríguez, L. and Vidal, E. (2007c). Computer Assisted Transcription for Ancient Text Images, in *International Conference on Image Analysis and Recognition, Lecture Notes in Computer Science,* Vol. 4633 (Springer-Verlag, Montreal (Canada)), pp. 1182–1193.

Romero, V., Toselli, A. H. and Vidal, E. (2009c). Using mouse feedback in computer assisted transcription of handwritten text images, in *Proceedings of the 10th International Conference on Document Analysis and Recognition,* IEEE Computer Society (Barcelona, Spain).

Romero, V., Toselli, A. H. and Vidal, E. (2010). Computer assisted transcription of text images: Results on the germana corpus and analysis of improvements needed for practical use, in *International Conference on Pattern Recognition* (Istanbul, Turkey), pp. 2017–2020.

Sankoff, D. and Kruskal, J. B. (1983). *Time Warps, String Edits, and Macromolecules: The Theory and Practice of Sequence Comparison* (Addisoin-Wesley).

SchlumbergerSema S.A., Instituto Tecnológico de Informática, Rheinisch

Westfälische Technische Hochschule Aachen Lehrstul für Informatik VI, Recherche Appliquée en Linguistique informatique Laboratory University of Montreal, Celer Soluciones and Societé Gamma and Xerox Research Centre Europe (2002-2005). TT2. TransType2 - computer assisted translation. in *Project technical annex. information Society Technologies (IST) Programme.*, IST-2001-32091.

Senior, A. and Robinson, A. (1998). An off-line cursive handwriting recognition system, *IEEE Transactions on Pattern Analysis and Machine Intelligence* **20**, 3, pp. 309–321.

Serrano, N. and Juan, A. (2010). The RODRIGO database, in *Proceedings of the The seventh international conference on Language Resources and Evaluation* (Malta), pp. 19–21.

Serrano, N., Sanchis, A. and Juan, A. (2010). Balancing error and supervision effort in interactive-predictive handwritten text recognition, in *Proceedings of the 15th International Conference on Intelligent User Interfaces* (Hong Kong (China)), pp. 373–376.

Shepard, D. H. (1953). Apparatus for reading, *US-Patent No 2663758* .

Srihari, S. (1993). Recognition of handwritten and machine printed text for postal adress interpretation, *Pattern Recognition Letters* **14**, pp. 291–302.

Srihari, S. N. and Keubert, E. J. (1997). Integration of handwritten address interpretation technology into the united states postal service remote computer reader system, in *Fourth International Conference Document Analysis and Recognition*, Vol. 2 (Ulm, Germany), pp. 892–896.

Stephens, M. (1974). EDF statistics for goodness of fit and some comparisons, *Journal of the American Statistical Association* **69**, 347, pp. 730–737.

Suhm, B., Myers, B. and Waibel, A. (2001). Multimodal Error Correction for Speech User Interfaces, *ACM Transactions on Computer-Human Interaction* **8**, 1, pp. 60–98.

Terrades, O. R., Toselli, A., Serrano, N., Romero, V., Vidal, E. and Juan, A. (2010). Interactive layout analysis and transcription systems for historic handwritten documents, in *10th ACM Symposium on Document Engineering*.

Tomás, J. and Casacuberta, F. (2006). Statistical phrase-based models for interactive computer-assisted translation, in *Proceedings of the Coling/ACL joint conference* (Sydney, Australia), pp. 835–841.

Toselli, A., Romero, V., Pastor, M. and Vidal, E. (2010). Multimodal interactive transcription of text images, *Pattern Recognition* **43**, 5, pp. 1824–1825.

Toselli, A. H. (2004). *Reconocimiento de Texto Manuscrito Continuo*, Ph.D. thesis, Departamento de Sistemas Informáticos y Computación. Universidad Politécnica de Valencia, Valencia (Spain), advisor(s): Dr. E. Vidal and Dr. A. Juan (in Spanish).

Toselli, A. H., Juan, A., Keysers, D., González, J., Salvador, I., H. Ney, Vidal, E. and Casacuberta, F. (2004a). Integrated Handwriting Recognition and Interpretation using Finite-State Models, *International Journal of Pattern Recognition and Artificial Intelligence* **18**, 4, pp. 519–539.

Toselli, A. H., Juan, A. and Vidal, E. (2004b). Spontaneous Handwriting Recognition and Classification, in *Proceedings of the 17th International Conference on Pattern Recognition*, Vol. 1 (Cambridge, United Kingdom), pp. 433–436.

Toselli, A. H., Romero, V., Rodríguez, L. and Vidal, E. (2007). Computer Assisted Transcription of Handwritten Text, in *9th International Conference on Document Analysis and Recognition* (IEEE Computer Society, Curitiba, Paraná (Brazil)), pp. 944–948.

Toselli, A. H., Romero, V. and Vidal, E. (2008). Computer assisted transcription of text images and multimodal interaction, in *Proceedings of the 5th Joint Workshop on Multimodal Interaction and Related Machine Learning Algorithms, Lecture Notes in Computer Science*, Vol. 5237 (Utrecht, The Netherlands), pp. 296–308.

Toselli, A. H., Vidal, E. and Casacuberta, F. (eds.) (2011). *Multimodal Interactive Pattern Recognition and Applications*, 1st edn. (Springer), http://www.springer.com/computer/hci/book/978-0-85729-478-4.

Tosellli, A. H., Pastor, M. and Vidal, E. (2007). On-Line Handwriting Recognition System for Tamil Handwritten Characters, in *3rd Iberian Conference on Pattern Recognition and Image Analysis, Lecture Notes in Computer Science (LNCS)*, Vol. 4477 (Springer-Verlag, Girona (Spain)), pp. 370–377.

Vidal, E., Casacuberta, F., Rodríguez, L., Civera, J. and Martínez, C. (2007a). Computer Assited Translation using speech Recognition. *IEEE Transaction on Audio, Speech and Language Processing* **14**, 3, pp. 941–951.

Vidal, E., Rodríguez, L., Casacuberta, F. and García-Varea, I. (2007b). Interactive pattern recognition, in *Proceedings of the 4th Joint Workshop on Multimodal Interaction and Related Machine Learning Algorithms, Lecture Notes in Computer Science*, Vol. 4892 (Brno, Czech Republic), pp. 60–71.

Vidal, E., Thollard, F., Casacuberta, F., de la Higuera, C. and Carrasco, R. (2005a). Probabilistic finite-state machines - part I, *IEEE Transactions on Pattern Analysis and Machine Intelligence* **27**, 7, pp. 1013–1025.

Vidal, E., Thollard, F., Casacuberta, F., de la Higuera, C. and Carrasco, R. (2005b). Probabilistic finite-state machines - part II, *IEEE Transactions on Pattern Analysis and Machine Intelligence* **27**, 7, pp. 1025–1039.

Vinciarelli, A. (2002). A survey on off-line cursive word recognition, *Pattern Recognition* **35**, 7, pp. 1033–1446.

Vuori, V., Laaksonen, J., Oja, E. and Kangas, J. (2001). Speeding Up On-line Recognition of Handwritten Characters by Pruning the Prototype Set, in *Proceedings of the Sixth International Conference on Document Analysis and Recognition* (Seattle, Washington), pp. 0501–0507.

Welling, L., Ney, H. and Kanthak, S. (2002). Speaker adaptive modeling by vocal tranc normalization, *IEEE Transactions on Speech and Audio Processing* **10**, pp. 415–426.

Witten, I. H. and Bell, T. C. (1991). The zero-frequency problem: Estimating the probabilities of novel events in adaptive text compression, *IEEE Transaction on Information Theory* **17**, 4.

Wong, K. Y., Casey, R. G. and Wahl, F. M. (1982). Document analysis system, *IBM Journal of Research and Development* **26**, 6, pp. 647–656.

Woodland, P. C. (2001). Speaker adaptation for continuous density hmms: A review, in *Proceedings of the ICSA workshop on adaptation methods for Speech Recognition* (Sophia, Antipolis, France).

Young, S., Odell, J., Ollason, D., Valtchev, V. and Woodland, P. (1997). *The HTK Book: Hidden Markov Models Toolkit V2.1*, Cambridge Research Laboratory Ltd.

Zimmermann, M. and Bunke, H. (2000). Automatic segmentation of the iam offline database for handwritten english text, in *In Proceedings of the 16th International Conference on Pattern Recognition*, Vol. 4, pp. 35–39.

Zimmermann, M., Chappelier, J.-C. and Bunke, H. (2006). Offline grammar-based recognition of handwritten sentences, *IEEE Transactions on Pattern Analysis and Machine Intelligence* **28**, 5, pp. 818–821, doi:http://dx.doi.org/10.1109/TPAMI.2006.103, member-Horst Bunke.

Index